PRAISE FOR

"If you want to unleash your full potential as a leader, read *Aligned* and learn how to focus on the highest value beliefs and actions that will both play to your unique strengths and help you shed the limiting distractions that may be holding you back. Hortense le Gentil is one of the most effective executive coaches in the world. *Aligned*, which is beautifully written and illustrated with memorable stories, puts her exclusive practice into a digestible form that will benefit any motivated professional aspiring to reach their highest potential as a leader."

JAMES M. CITRIN, LEADER, SPENCER STUART CEO PRACTICE AND AUTHOR, THE CAREER PLAYBOOK

"*Aligned* opens new doors for anyone wanting to lead with ease, joy and impact."

FRANCES HESSELBEIN, PRESIDENTIAL MEDAL OF FREEDOM RECIPIENT, EDITOR-IN-CHIEF, *LEADER TO LEADER JOURNAL*, FORMER CEO, GIRL SCOUTS OF THE USA

"In her brilliant new book, *Aligned*, Hortense le Gentil shows how to perform at your peak as a leader in today's volatile world: align your authentic self in mind, body, and spirit with your 'why' and then align your team with their 'why' around a common mission and values. With challenging reflections, le Gentil provides a roadmap to your sustained success as an authentic and aligned leader."

BILL GEORGE, SENIOR FELLOW, HARVARD BUSINESS SCHOOL, FORMER CHAIR AND CEO, MEDTRONIC, AND AUTHOR OF *DISCOVER YOUR TRUE NORTH*

"Hortense le Gentil provides an invaluable set of practical approaches for anyone, including experienced and aspiring leaders, who desires to unleash their full potential."

ARNOLD W. DONALD, CEO, CARNIVAL CORPORATION

"In *Aligned*, Hortense le Gentil leverages her experience as one of the world's foremost executive coaches to take us on a journey to explore who we are, who we want to be, and how to get there. This book is a must-read for anyone who wants to become a better leader."

DR. TASHA EURICH, *NEW YORK TIMES* BESTSELLING AUTHOR OF *INSIGHT* AND *BANKABLE LEADERSHIP*

"This is a beautiful and insightful book. Hortense offers healthy doses of clarity in a form that's easy to swallow. She helps each of us find and hold onto our truths, even when chaos swirls around us."

FIONA M. MACAULAY, FOUNDER-CEO, WILD NETWORK, WOMEN INNOVATORS & LEADERS DEVELOPMENT

"Realizing the connection between who you truly are and your core strategy, is what you need to achieve everything you want and realize your true potential! *Aligned* is THE book to find your perfect recipe to connect your true self with the right path to your success!"

GREGORY RENARD, HEAD OF ARTIFICIAL INTELLIGENCE AT xBRAIN, HEAD OF APPLIED AI & SDS AT NASA FDL

ALIGNED

ALIGNED

Connecting Your True Self with the Leader You're Meant to Be

HORTENSE LE GENTIL

PAGE TWO
BOOKS

ISBN 978-1-989025-90-1 (paperback)
ISBN 978-1-989025-91-8 (ebook)

Produced by Page Two
www.pagetwo.com

Edited by Paul Taunton
Cover design by Emanuel Ilagan
Interior design by Taysia Louie

www.hortenselegentil.com

To Greg and Charlotte.

You give me joy and energy! Remember to always be positive, follow your dreams, and stay aligned!

With all my love.

CONTENTS

FOREWORD

IN ALIGNED, Hortense le Gentil shares with us the incredibly important concept of alignment as it relates to life and leadership, from her perspective as a leadership coach whose work is based on the human dimension of leadership.

Hortense compares *alignment* to being on a roll. Think of those moments when time slows, and you see everything clearly. Past the noise and distractions, you zoom in on the essential and instinctively know what to do. An athlete (Hortense was once a competitive show-jumper) might say you are "in the zone," like a surfer riding the perfect wave. As she puts it, "Alignment is ... about becoming more of yourself—and in so doing, transcending what you thought were the limits of your capabilities."

I very much relate to this description of alignment. So much so that one of my books, *Mojo*, is about this very subject. When I talk of 'mojo,' I mean "that positive spirit toward what we are doing now that starts from the inside and radiates to the outside." This is very similar to Hortense's view—that self-motivation spurs us onward to achieve for ourselves as well as for others.

I think the concept of alignment is very important—the fact that the leader has to make sure that the larger goals of the organization are connected to the goals of the subgroup and the team and the individual. In *Aligned*, Hortense takes this idea to a whole other level. And she talks about it in a unique and refreshing way, which I love.

She stresses how alignment relates to all of us as people, and how that personal alignment is just as important as professional alignment. This concept is essential for the leader of the future. Our work is such an important part of our lives today, and you can't separate that other person from the leader.

The leader of the future faces five key challenges—and alignment helps with all of them. First, they are going to have to think globally, not just locally. Leadership is a whole lot different when you're managing around the world, and the concept of alignment takes on a whole new level of importance when it's global. The second challenge, cross-cultural diversity—not just between women and men but across cultures—is similar. Alignment is easy when everyone is like you—when you're in a world where everyone *isn't* like you it becomes a much bigger challenge, and even more important.

Third, future leaders will have to have tech savvy. In a world where everything is changing so rapidly, the leader has to understand that, and work to keep people aligned with the new technology. That's a whole lot more challenging than when technology is stable. Fourth, leaders have to understand how to build alliances and partnerships. Leadership used to be much more top-down; now it's going to be much more across. That's what alignment is about, whether it's building alliances with your partners, suppliers, even sometimes with your competitors. The concept of alignment is very closely allied to building alliances and partnerships.

And finally, that leader of the future is going to have to be a facilitator, much more than an expert who tells people what to do and how to do it. When you manage knowledge experts, you can't tell them, you have to be a facilitator who helps them. If you know what to do and how to do it, alignment is easy. In a world where you're not the expert, where you don't know everything, you need to involve people. The alignment becomes more challenging—and much, much more important.

One of life's irrefutable laws is, know yourself, and anything is possible. Hortense shows us how to let go of our restrictions and old beliefs, so we can learn to behave and think differently, align our values with our actions, and learn from past experiences. As I always say, what was right yesterday may be not right tomorrow.

With *Aligned*, you will learn, practice, and become who you want to be. As a leader you will become agile and focused on your purpose and passion and as a human being you will become the person you want to be at the highest level!

Life is good.

MARSHALL GOLDSMITH

INTRODUCTION

HAVE YOU EVER felt like you were on a roll? Every thing seems to be going your way. Time slows, and you see clearly. Past the noise and distractions, you're able to zoom in on the essential. You take the perfect action at the perfect time, like Neo effortlessly dodging bullets in *The Matrix*. You instinctively know what to do, and you have the profound feeling that you are on the right path. Perhaps you have even experienced what many athletes describe as being "in the flow" or "in the zone." Surfers catch the perfect wave, and skiers effortlessly navigate challenging slaloms. That state of consciousness where we feel in the groove and perform at the optimal level is not the prerogative of a chosen few but is available to everyone.

This experience is the manifestation of what I call *alignment*. Alignment is the congruence of who you are, what you feel, and what you love on a deep and fundamental level with what you do, what you say, what you envision, and where you are going. Alignment is not about falling in step or conforming to others' expectations, but rather it's about becoming more yourself—and, in so doing, transcending what you thought were the limits of your capabilities.

Think of your spine. When all your vertebrae are working as they should, stacked in perfect position on top of each other and flexing across their full range of motion without constriction, that alignment benefits your entire body via the multitude of nerves connected to them. Any constriction or blockage in any part of your spine, on the other hand, and the chain reaction works in the other direction: your body experiences pain, friction, a narrower range of movement, or lower energy. In short, it operates below its potential.

I experienced alignment firsthand as a teenager when I was a competitive show jumper: the perfect communion with my horse, the clear vision of how to navigate the obstacle course, and the laser focus on what needs to be done—free of the noise of thoughts and doubts. I felt seamless communication with the horse through hands and legs, using anticipation, intuitive agility, and subtle adjustments to stay in perfect balance—producing a sense of ease, clarity, calmness, and effortless power. I became one with my horse, and together we became one with the whole, transcending limitations.

I come from a family with a long tradition of horse breeding and competitive jumping, and horsemanship has been running in our blood for generations. I was riding horses by the time I was four years old and competing by age ten.

It is therefore hardly surprising that I learned a lot about alignment from horseback riding—and that equestrian examples run through these pages. I later applied these lessons to a corporate career in marketing and communication, and again when I created a business in the steel recycling industry. Those experiences and what I learned through them have coalesced into leadership coaching and public speaking, and today I help top executives and entrepreneurs become even better at what they do by finding—and maintaining—their alignment. Time and again, I witness how they are then able to step up their performance with ease and joy and successfully embrace new challenges. Their sense of alignment facilitates the agility, speed, and foresight that are essential to navigate increasingly complex environments, rapid change, and uncertainty. By fully becoming the leaders they are meant to be, they are more influential and broaden their reach as well as their impact, leaping from successful to extraordinary.

The leader in you is no different. You too, if properly aligned, can reach higher than you ever thought possible, effortlessly and joyfully inspiring others to embrace and follow your vision. You too can generate that sense of clarity and ease, even in the face of challenges and setbacks. You too can create that congruence of who you are, what you think, and what you do.

Alignment does not happen by itself, however. It requires a willingness to connect with who you truly are, to do the work to become who you want to be, and to project your aligned self from your inner world onto the outside one.

It requires the courage to disrupt your own status quo. It requires the right tools and guidance to bust through your self-limitations.

How do you generate that sense of alignment? That is what this book is about. It is a manual to get you started. What lies in these pages has emerged from my own experience and from coaching dozens of leaders from a variety of industries over the years, greatly enriched by my participation in the Marshall Goldsmith's 100 Coaches project. The MG100, as it is known, is the extraordinary group gathered by the number-one *New York Times* bestselling author of *Triggers*, *MOJO*, and *What Got You Here Won't Get You There*, Marshall Goldsmith to "pay it forward" and teach everything he knows for free, provided the participants teach others themselves. I have been immensely privileged to be part of that journey, which has helped me refine my thinking on alignment. This book focuses on leadership in a broad sense—whether you are the CEO of a multinational or of your own life.

At the core of this book and of my work as a coach is the human dimension of leadership: alignment deals with emotional intelligence in service of your relationship with both yourself and others. This book rests on the concept of the leader as a coach-in-chief who steers a ship with influence. This concept has been written about extensively, and my purpose here is to build on it by illustrating how it connects with alignment. This book is also built on the premise that organizations are made of the hearts and minds of the many people who orbit within their area of influence, from employees to suppliers, customers, and local communities.

Part I is about connecting with yourself—identifying your purpose, your values, and what self-limitations might be standing in your way—to delineate and highlight your alignment gap. Part II offers tools to narrow that gap and better align yourself with the purpose and values you've identified, while busting your self-limitations. Part III focuses on how to project your new inner alignment outward to facilitate the collective alignment of people around you, boosting your influence and impact as a leader. Finally, the conclusion brings it all together and offers a practice of daily questions to help you stay—or get back—on track. Chapters build upon each other in sequence, but each also stands alone for the browsers among you who would rather dip in and out of this book.

Are you ready for the journey towards authentic and aligned leadership? If so, read on!

PART ONE

Meet Yourself

"Are you ready
to take a good look
at yourself?"

———————

PETER DRUCKER, the world-renowned management consultant, argued that having clarity on who we are is essential if we want to manage our professional trajectory effectively. The same is true with authentic, aligned leadership. Unless we are fully aware of who we truly are, we cannot find alignment. Why? Because we do not know what to align with.

"Of course I know who I am!" you may think. And, of course, you're right. In many ways you do know who you are. Yet in reality, most of us tend to have a surprisingly restricted, inaccurate, or incomplete knowledge of ourselves. We all have blind spots that make us unable to identify some of our strengths, weaknesses, and values as well as the self-limitations that slow us down. Or, focused on the demands of our daily lives, we do not fully keep up with how we change and grow over time, and the way we view ourselves becomes outdated.

Alignment therefore starts with being authentically connected with who you are, what you want, and your deeper sense of purpose, as well as your unique strengths and values. Knowing who you are also means acknowledging what you could improve upon and the obstacles that stand in your way.

What lessons have you learned from your triumphs and setbacks? What are your specific talents? What deeper purpose drives you to do what you do? What values do you care deeply about? What impact do you want to have? These form the foundation of who you are. This is your benchmark and your point of reference—the GPS coordinates of your destination.

The chapters in Part I guide you through this journey of self-discovery, or rediscovery, to highlight your alignment gap. You'll first get a glimpse of typical symptoms of misalignment, before being introduced to how coaching can facilitate your journey towards alignment. Then you'll delineate your purpose, clarify your values and qualities, examine your life, and identify your self-limitations.

Are you ready to take a good look at yourself?

1

MIND THE GAP

THERE ARE TWO kinds of equestrians: those who seek to impose their will onto their horse, muscling their way forward and pulling on the reins; and those who seek to work in harmony and alignment with their horse, cultivating mutual trust, ease, and communication. Both can be successful. The first, however, is more likely to hit a ceiling. Why? Because imposing your will requires force and therefore far more energy, both of which go only so far. It triggers friction if not outright resistance, and equestrians who rely on it are likely to get either outwilled or outweighed by their 1,300-pound horse. The second kind of rider, on the other hand, is in a much better position to keep stretching the boundaries of their potential—as well as their horse's. When working in authentic harmony, force is no longer necessary: instead of resisting, the horse gives more and responds better and more quickly to the rider.

These equestrians and their horses become far nimbler, able to adjust their course of action when necessary, refine their skills, and ultimately leap farther, all while experiencing the highs of alignment.

Psychiatrist David Hawkins distinguishes force—which he defines as a movement that invariably results in a counterforce—from power, or the ability to inspire others to follow you. Force creates friction, resistance, and polarization, and its impact is therefore limited. Force also inherently creates conflicts and win/lose situations, which are costly. Hawkins argues that power, on the other hand, is like gravity: it moves everything within its field but is itself still. Power arises from meaning and significance, inspiring what is noble and uplifting within human nature. Power generates energy. And power requires alignment.

Which kind of person are you? Do you rely more on power or on force? Are you equipped to handle the next challenge, step into a new role, or navigate unexpected changes with ease? Or are you like a Ferrari driving in second gear, with horsepower remaining unused?

And how do you know if you are aligned or not? What are the signs?

Mark,[1] a top corporate executive, had built a very successful career on the back of his outstanding technical skills. Thanks to his expertise, he had climbed corporate echelon after corporate echelon. Yet his own CEO felt Mark was not ready for the next promotion. Why? Because Mark was disconnected from his peers, often unable to convince them to adopt his ideas, no matter how brilliant. His own team was

Alignment will make it a lot easier to tackle the unavoidable obstacles and challenges that keep cropping up.

---

performing but without enthusiasm, a sense of initiative, or purpose—content to wait for him to pass down instructions. In short, Mark was unable to unleash the true extent of his power. Without realizing it, he had hit a ceiling.

Sheryl, on the other hand, found it easy to get the best out of her team. People in the corporate finance department she managed loved working for her, feeling valued and consistently fired up. Sheryl exuded competence and provided a clear sense of direction. Yet she felt hemmed in: she excelled at what she did, but she was frustrated to be relegated to a function that did not capitalize on her creativity. Her peers and her boss seemed to have pigeonholed her, unable to see and appreciate the full extent of her talents. And this was getting in the way of further advancement.

To step into
a new role you
need a different
approach that
taps into a
different part
of yourself.

As for Robert, the respect that his competence, hard work, and results commanded was undermined by his belligerence towards people around him, with whom he was in perpetual conflict. Robert always kept his guard up, trusting no one and expecting betrayal and duplicity from his colleagues. His coworkers walked on eggshells, weary of the unavoidable battles. Every decision was hard-fought and second-guessed. Unbeknownst to Robert himself, this absorbed much of his energy and focus, leaving him exhausted and on edge.

When Gary was unexpectedly pushed into early retirement after a successful career straddling the public and the private sectors, he had no idea what to do. He was unprepared for this sudden change, and for the first time in years his next step was unclear. Long absorbed by the demands of his work and daily life, he had not spent any time reflecting on his retirement, and the thought that his work life could be over was a source of anxiety. Who was he stripped of his professional status, without collaborators, assistants, meetings and responsibilities?

Do you recognize yourself in Mark, Sheryl, Robert, or Gary? Perhaps, like Mark, what has worked for you so far is no longer sufficient. To step into a new role, sit on the board, propel the company you've created, or just generally step up your game, you need a different approach that taps into a different part of yourself—and you're not sure how best to find it. Or, like Sheryl, your current role does not fully match who you are and the full spectrum of your talents and strengths. Or maybe you keep facing the same situations or falling back on the same behavior, and, like Robert, you're not sure why or how to break the pattern. Or perhaps you relate most closely to Gary: you're facing an important decision, and instead of clarity about your best way forward, what you're feeling is closer to confusion, doubt, and anxiety.

You could also be like many of my other clients, who have been very successful yet feel they could be more so. Or, without knowing exactly why, you cannot shake off a vague sense of discontent. A lingering sense of frustration. A lack of energy and enthusiasm. A chronic short fuse. Pervasive anxiety. Inexplicable chronic pain. Or you don't remember the last time you had a good night's sleep or went through the day without feeling as though you're wearing lead boots. Perhaps, by all measures, you've reached the top of the mountain, fulfilling what you've been working towards for so long: you've made the money, gotten the top job, received the award, or sold the company—take your pick. Yet you're feeling disappointed. Somehow that success is not bringing you all the fulfillment you were hoping for. All the boxes have been ticked, so why aren't you ecstatic? What's missing?

What you sense is a gap between who you are and what you truly want. What's missing is alignment with yourself, and you're in need of a tune-up.

Don't get me wrong. I'm not suggesting that after you read this book, every challenge and pain will vanish, so you can live happily ever after, feeling like a superhero. Being aligned does not mean that the road suddenly becomes clear all the time. Will you still face tough problems once in a while? Yes. Will you still make mistakes and will you still face conflicts? Absolutely. And you will certainly still feel tired when you don't get enough sleep or have traveled across ten time zones.

So, you may ask, why am I reading this book? Because alignment will make it a lot easier to tackle the unavoidable obstacles and challenges that keep cropping up. When aligned with your authentic self, decisions become a lot easier, because the perspective you've gained allows you to see better. You're able to do more, spending less energy; you feel a sense of peace even in tough situations, knowing in your bones that you're on the right path, confident in your ability to handle everything coming your way. You have become that finely tuned Ferrari working on *all* cylinders, moving into top gear when required.

That is alignment.

For now, ask yourself: how far do you feel from it? Where is your own gap, and how wide does it feel?

Next, we'll explore how coaching can help you close that gap and facilitate your journey towards alignment.

REFLECTIONS:

How Aligned Are You?

never: 0   sometimes: -1   often: -2   very often: -3

1. Do you overreact to situations?
2. Do you feel chronic pain?
3. Are you always in a hurry?
4. Do you wake up in a bad mood?
5. Are you aggressive?
6. Do you feel sad?
7. Do you blame others?
8. Do you feel drained?

Your negative score total =

never: 0   sometimes: +1   often: +2   very often: +3

1. Do you experience joy with your family, friends, or coworkers?
2. Do you laugh?
3. Do you feel happy?
4. Do you feel free?
5. Do you sleep well?
6. Are you the decision-maker in your life?
7. Are you positive?
8. Does your life give you energy?

Your positive score total =

Do you want to improve your alignment by increasing your positive score and/or decreasing your negative one?

2

MIRROR, MIRROR
ON THE WALL

LOOK DOWN AT your own body. You can see your front and your sides. But can you see the top of your head? Your back? Your forehead? Not unless you have a mirror or two. The same is true when we examine our inner selves. Some parts we see clearly, but others remain entirely out of sight, regardless of how much we want to view them.

A coach is like a mirror. Their role is to illuminate parts of yourself that you cannot see, offering perspective and awareness, and to help you reach beyond what you think you can do. The value of coaching is well understood in sports. Usain Bolt, the Olympic gold medal winning sprinter, remembers what Glen Mills, the former head coach of Jamaica's national team, used to tell him whenever he doubted himself. "Don't worry," his coach would say. "I know what I can do to make you run faster and what you need to do to go faster."[1]

I experienced the immense benefits of coaching from an early age. When I was a competitive show jumper on the Northern France regional junior equestrian team, I had two coaches: my father and Charlotte Masquelier. They made sure my horse and I trained properly to develop the right muscles and impeccable technique. In addition to guiding my physical training, they helped me work on my mindset. My father and I debriefed after each race. If I'd done well, he would help me build on my success and focus on the next challenge. If, on the other hand, I was angry and disappointed, he would help me regain perspective and learn from my mistakes. As an outside observer, Charlotte was able to point out what I could not see and how I could improve my performance. She was always there for me, listening, understanding, knowing when to push me hard or lighten the pressure with a joke at the right moment. She kept me focused. When I felt I was at the top of my game, she showed me how I could go higher still, when I could not see it myself. Whenever I felt discouraged, frustrated, or demotivated, she reminded me why I was doing this, finding the right words to gently steer me back on track. The admiration and gratitude she inspired in me were so great that I named my daughter after her.

Premier athletes rely on a trusted, top-notch coach: in fact, they often rely on an entire support team. Would

Rafael Nadal or the Williams sisters have become tennis champions without a coach helping them develop their talent and fulfill their potential? Not a chance. Did they decide they no longer needed coaching when they became successful? Absolutely not. Research from the Institute for the Psychology of Elite Performance at Bangor University in the UK suggests that one of the key differences between a gold medalist—known as a super-elite athlete—and those in the next tier of top athletes is their relationship with their coach. Beyond providing technical and tactical support, coaches of the super-elite develop a close relationship with their athletes and in doing so are able to encourage, motivate, and provide emotional support to get the best out of them.[2] So inspiring is the power of a good coach that it has become central to countless sports movies, such as Clint Eastwood's *Million Dollar Baby* and *Remember the Titans* with Denzel Washington.

Every athlete knows that, regardless of how successful they are, they can always keep getting better at what they do. They know that their sport is both a technical game and an inner game, each requiring not only practice and determination but continued coaching. This is what inspired surgeon and writer Atul Gawande to conduct an experiment. For the first five years after he started practicing surgery, Gawande kept learning and improving in the operating room. Honing his skills through practice, his complication rate steadily declined. But then his learning curve plateaued. That's when he decided to test whether the benefits of coaching applied to his field.

Premier athletes rely on a trusted, top-notch coach: in fact, they often rely on an entire support team.

Gawande invited one of his former professors to observe his surgeries right in the operating room. The first surgery went very well, so Gawande expected that his professor/coach would have little to say. Instead, the professor had lots of notes. Because he could observe from a distance, he was able to notice many small, simple things that Gawande could not see, such as the position of his elbow or a light slightly out of place. It turns out that these minor adjustments can make a significant difference. "It was a whole other level of awareness," remembers Gawande. After two months of this regimen, his complication rate started improving again. This led him to conclude that the role of the coach is to be "your external eyes and ears, providing a more accurate picture of your reality."[3]

Leadership is no different. Executive coaching might not have quite the same cinematic pull as boxing or football, but top executives are in many ways like top athletes: they strive to be the best at what they do. But without someone offering an informed perspective, they can only go so far. Business leadership has become decreasingly about technical expertise and increasingly about embracing rapid change in a global environment. The notion that everyone, including surgeons and CEOs, can stretch further and perform better, no matter how good they already are, is making headway outside the sporting world. Studies have confirmed that coaching improves how individuals function in organizations, with significant positive effects on performance, skills, well-being, coping, work attitude, and goal-directed self-regulation.[4] "Everyone needs a coach," affirms Bill Gates. "Get a coach," Scott Cook, the founder of Intuit, advised fresh graduates from Harvard Business School. Google, Pepsi, HP, NASA—all have embraced executive coaching. IBM trains, certifies, and develops its own team of internal business coaches, which currently includes more than 1,000 people, and coaching is a new way of leading and working within the company. Jennifer Paylor, for instance, joined IBM as a gaming software developer/engineer when she was nineteen years old but became a People Engineer who now leads the IBM global coaching practice.[5]

Many executives still do not get proper coaching, however, considering it a sign of weakness, a remedial measure, like tutoring for students who fall behind. Why would top CEOs need coaching? After all, they're extraordinarily successful and experts at what they do. They've made a career out of effectively tackling complex challenges, right?

This is what Eric Schmidt, the former CEO of Google, thought when a board member suggested a coach. "I don't need a coach," he said. "I'm an established CEO. Why would I need a coach? Is something wrong?" But then he gave it a try and came to understand that we can all benefit from a trusted pair of eyes to get perspective on ourselves and our actions. He now recalls that recommendation as the best advice he ever got.[6]

Hubert Joly, chairman and CEO of Best Buy, traveled a similar path. Although he regularly worked with coaches to improve his tennis game and skiing technique, work was somehow different. He struggled to take constructive feedback, instead finding fault in the person who offered it. He used to believe that executives who turned to coaching were in some way deficient. But that changed when Joly was introduced to Marshall Goldsmith. Once he realized that Goldsmith's coaching clients were highly successful leaders—that there was nothing "wrong" with them—his view changed. Instead of resisting feedback as something that highlighted problems, he could embrace it as an opportunity to become even better at what he did; just as with tennis or skiing, Joly learned that an effective leader does not have to be the smartest person in the room and be in charge of everything.[7]

To varying degrees, we're all encumbered by our inner selves saying, "I cannot," or "I should not." We're hemmed in by limitations we've put in our own way; often, we do not

———

We can all use some coaching to get us running on all cylinders and leaping forward as a more aligned version of ourselves.

———

see them at all. And if we do, we don't always know how to get past them. We need help.

So, you're successful? You could be even more so and accelerate your career, once you get clarity and tackle what's keeping you back. We can all use some coaching to get us running on all cylinders and leaping forward as a more aligned version of ourselves.

Now that we've discussed how coaching can support you on your way towards better alignment, let's explore what guides and anchors that very journey.

3

CONNECT WITH
YOUR "WHY"

WHY DO YOU do what you do? What makes you get out of bed in the morning? What drives you to keep going when confronted with obstacles or setbacks? There are practical answers to these questions. You have a career or your own business, and you want to keep being successful. Or you're on your way to getting that corner office. Perhaps you're already there and you want to keep it. But I'm not asking about superficial answers: I'm asking about a deeper, broader sense of purpose, bigger than yourself.

I'm asking about your "why."

Many years ago, what drove future Best Buy chairman and CEO Hubert Joly was a relentless pursuit of perfection. Always an excellent student, he joined a top consulting firm

Aligning that personal "why" with a company's purpose can unleash extraordinary performance.

---

after graduation, and his ambition was clear. "For me, life was about achieving perfection," he explains. "In my mind, consciously or not, this was how I was going to live my life: achieve success and be happy." He used to believe his role as a leader was to have all the answers. Case closed. Or so he thought.

Early in his career, conversations with a monk and a client CEO first put Joly on the path to what he now calls "purposeful leadership." Tasked with turning around struggling companies, he searched for a deeper sense of purpose. He came to understand the importance of what drives us at a deep level—how aligning that personal "why" with a company's purpose can unleash extraordinary performance, particularly in very challenging circumstances. Joly's personal drive became about having a positive impact on the people around him and using the power of his platform to contribute to the common good. Perhaps not what you'd expect from someone considered a turnaround expert. Yet, this clear sense of purpose is part of what has made Joly a successful leader.

Why should you focus on your "why"? Because without a clear "why" to guide one's choices, it is much easier to get lost: have you ever pursued something that you thought you wanted—the next work project, the shinier job, the fatter paycheck—only to realize when you got there that it left you disappointed? We all get influenced by our environment, the people around us, and off-the-shelf, one-size-fits-all images of success, instead of tailoring our own idea of success to fit our exact measurements. In addition, leaders who do not properly connect with the meaning and purpose behind their actions find it far more difficult to stay the course when the going gets tough. Finally, the best leaders inspire others to act and follow in their wake by articulating a "why." We'll discuss this further in Part III.

Bestselling author and leadership consultant Simon Sinek, who has studied how great leaders inspire action, explains the power of "why" through what he calls the "golden circle."[1] Sinek's golden circle comprises three concentric parts. The "what"—what you do—is the outer circle. Most people know exactly what they do: they sell computers, for example, or they lead companies. The second level in is the "how"—how you do what you do, and how you do it differently or better than others. Most people and companies communicate by focusing on the "what" and the "how." They sell computers with more functionality or that are cheaper. CEOs maximize shareholder value. The problem is the "what" and "how" by themselves are not very inspiring.

The bull's-eye at the very center of the golden circle is the "why"—the bigger purpose, the reason why others care. Sinek argues that few people have a good grasp of their "why." But if they manage to identify this wider vision and connect it with the "how" and the "what," they are more likely to inspire others to follow. This is because the "why" appeals to the non-verbal part of our brain, which involves our feelings, memories, motivation, and behavior. "People don't buy what you do," Sinek concludes. "They buy *why* you do it."

If you want to unleash that phenomenal power as a leader, start by getting clarity on what really drives you. Do you have a good handle on your own "why"? If it is only about advancing your career, making more money for shareholders, or selling more widgets, you might find it hard to be an inspiring leader. Instead, look deeper to find your connection with a more universal, higher purpose that others can share. This is what makes people want to work for and with you and to give their very best when they do. Knowing your deeper "why" will also make decisions easier for you, as they can be measured against the yardstick of that higher purpose.

It starts with you. If you're not clear on what your own "why" is, how can you tell if it aligns with what you do or with what your company does? You can't. How can you

If you want to
unleash that
phenomenal power
as a leader, start
by getting clarity
on what really
drives you.

communicate it effectively? You can't. How can you convince others driven by the same purpose to follow you? You can't. Your "why" is what Bill George,[2] former CEO of Medtronic who teaches leadership at Harvard Business School, calls your "true north."

More often than not, however, defining this true north is easier said than done. Caught up in our daily lives, we rarely take time to stop and ask ourselves what fundamentally drives us to do the work we do. Almost all of my coaching clients face this. Perhaps they once thought they knew, but then things changed. Or they changed.

So, where do you start (or start again)?

You start at the beginning. What was your childhood dream? What did you want to become?

As children, we don't need to know who we are; we just are. While our brains are still under construction, anything seems possible to us. But later we get influenced by events, our environment, and the opinions of others, all of which shape our sense of what's possible. Our prefrontal cortex, responsible for complex decision-making and impulse control, develops as we grow; as we become more rational and better at self-control, we also lose spontaneity and develop inhibitions. We become more "reasonable" and dream smaller. Sometimes, we even stop dreaming at all. Yet dreams often carry the seed of our "why." They power our achievements. They are the emotional fuel that gives us purpose and propels us forward, feeding our desire to go further. Dreams strengthen our resilience and provide fresh ideas, so we can rebound when faced with adversity.

Am I saying that you should drop everything and become the firefighter or pop singer you once dreamed you would become? No. The purpose here is to look for clues and then zoom in on what it was in those early aspirations that gave you life. The point is to find ways to adapt and integrate that life-giving, chest-expanding energy back into yourself and find its broader meaning.

Growing up, Estelle wanted to be a schoolteacher. She never became one. When she started working with me, she was running her own tech company and leading workshops, helping other businesses turn digital. In working together, she realized her purpose had in fact not changed at all. She was still driven by the same desire to share knowledge and to help others grow and learn something new. Her business was in perfect alignment with her "why." Being able to see it and articulate it gave her a clearer focus, sharpened her communication, and made decisions much easier, because she could test the choices that she faced against her "why" and make sure they were in alignment.

If you dreamed of becoming a doctor, chances are you are keen to help others heal. Some of my clients' dreams of becoming soccer stars revealed their penchant for working towards collective achievement as well as for competition. If old childhood dreams have long been forgotten, or nothing in them speaks to you any longer, look for a more recent one. If you could do anything, what would you do, and why?

Whatever the dream is, step back from the specifics, identify its building blocks, and rearrange them in a configuration appropriate for where you are today. Have you found ways to integrate these elements into your life, or can you still do so?

As a teenager, George dreamed of becoming a film director. Then life got in the way. He had to make a living quickly, and instead of stepping behind a camera, he sat behind a desk. Along the way he forgot his initial dream. Fast-forward five decades or so: he's now in his sixties. Recently sidelined from his company, he's lost track of where he wanted to go and what was important to him. What should he do next? Where to start?

We took a closer look at why George had wanted to be a director all those years ago. What drove him was the desire to tell visual stories that would highlight social challenges, bring people together, and make a positive difference in the world. Did he drop everything to become the next Martin Scorsese? No. He found ways to adapt and integrate that energy into what he would do next. It turns out that, without realizing it, he had in fact borrowed some elements of his old dream and made them part of his life after all. Throughout his career, he had been an exceptional communicator, often relying on stories to advance his arguments and convince people. While working in public service, he had also gotten involved in pressing social challenges. Once his "why" came into sharper focus, he found additional ways to bring those elements and more into his life. He took on a role in an NGO, facilitating integration in inner cities. He then decided to publish a book, which he wrote as he would have a screenplay, thinking cinematically.

Not everyone loses track of their "why." Perhaps you have fully realized your initial aspirations, but it is now time to pivot, while still holding on to what has been driving you all along. Top athletes, for instance, often find themselves in this situation when they reach the end of their career in competition, which is typically still early in their lives.

Taking a good look at your dreams is one way to reconnect with yourself and find clues about what drives you. It illuminates your personal, unique "why"—that sense of purpose larger than yourself.

Sophie had a very successful career in public service, but she was not clear on what lay behind her choice. As we worked together, she revealed that her parents had fled their home country and found refuge in France, which had saved their lives. She has now realized that what drives her is to protect, sustain, and advance the institutions of a liberal democracy. Getting that clarity has given her a deep sense of alignment with her career choice. It has also unleashed a powerful emotional charge that helps her project a deeper meaning and, as Simon Sinek puts it, communicate from the inside out. In other words, it has helped her become a more inspiring leader.

But what you do professionally may not be congruent with what you care deeply about. Paul, in charge of public relations for an insurance association, spent most of his days lobbying government bodies on behalf of financial institutions. Although he excelled at what he did, he lacked genuine enthusiasm for it, which drained his energy. Working together, we identified that he disliked the political aspect of his role. What motivated him was to directly influence ordinary people's lives through services at the operational level. With his purpose clarified, he was able to leave his position and pivot to a senior operational role in a company that serves individuals.

Consider also that what might have felt right for you at one stage in your life may no longer. We change and evolve, as do our circumstances and the world around us. Through our life experiences, we ideally learn more about who we are and refine our path accordingly. For some of us, our "why" might remain broadly the same, but its manifestation may evolve. My own teenage dream of becoming an Olympic champion morphed into something different as I grew older, and I decided to embark on a different path.

So, let me ask you again: why do you do what you do? What makes you get out of bed in the morning? What drives you to keep going when confronted with obstacles or setbacks? What's your "why"?

Perhaps you're not clear yet. Stay with it. Mull over it. If you have not thought about it for a while—or ever—it may take time to get clarity. Hold on to these questions as you go through the next chapters: while you work on your alignment from additional angles, you're likely to glean more clues to help you zoom in on your "why."

REFLECTIONS

What was your childhood dream? Think about why. What in that dream gave you life?

_____

_____

_____

_____

What are the major elements of that dream? How did you integrate them, or some of them, into your life? And if you have not, how could you still do so? Be specific.

_____

_____

_____

_____

In what way is what your profession congruent with what you care deeply about?

_____

_____

_____

_____

How would you define your purpose, your driver, your "why"?

_____

_____

_____

If you could do anything, what would you do?

_____

_____

_____

4

WHO DO YOU ASPIRE TO BE?

WHAT ARE YOUR main qualities? What personality traits best define you? In other words, what makes you uniquely who you are? What values matter most to you, and how do you manifest them?

Are you able to answer these questions with clarity and certainty? Not so easy, is it? First, these are broad, rather abstract questions. Second, we are not always able to see ourselves all that objectively, and rarely do we see ourselves the way others perceive us. If you've ever been the subject of a 360 assessment, chances are you were at least partly surprised by how your colleagues, team, or bosses described you. They might have identified your main qualities as traits you didn't even realize about yourself, or you might have felt a tad defensive (or been in full-blown denial) about areas you need to improve. To muddy the waters even more, we don't always fully express our true selves or who we would like to be.

To move towards inner alignment, however, requires us to first get clarity on these questions. If a direct approach is not all that useful, how can we get clearer answers about ourselves?

Years ago, I used to watch *Bouillon de culture*, a very popular French cultural talk show. Bernard Pivot, the host, always asked the same ten questions of his guest. What is your favorite word? And your least favorite? What about curse words? What noise do you love, and which do you hate? And so on. The questions themselves seemed innocuous, even random. Yet every time, without fail, what the answers—and the discussion that invariably followed— revealed about the guests was extraordinary. Each question was like a key unlocking a door to their thoughts, values, and beliefs. By the end of the show, viewers had been given an authentic portrait of whoever had been interviewed.

For those of you more familiar with American television, James Lipton, longtime host of *Inside the Actors Studio*, based his own questionnaire on Bernard Pivot's. Pivot himself had been inspired by a questionnaire that French novelist Marcel Proust answered at age thirteen and then again at age twenty (a questionnaire popularized in the United States by *Vanity Fair*). Even though Pivot's own questions were different, the principle was exactly the same: when it comes to delineating who we truly are, peripheral approaches are often far more enlightening than direct ones.

Childhood dreams, covered in the previous chapter, have already provided some clues about true identity. Besides offering a path to uncovering your "why," the qualities of the professional aspirations you once had (or still nurture) also illuminate what you value most—and are therefore part of who you are. One of my clients, for example, once dreamed of becoming a fighter pilot. Why? Because to him, it meant speed, adrenaline, and altitude. Even though that specific profession was no longer relevant to him, he still very much valued the qualities he once associated with it. They still defined him.

Let's add questions to make up our own Proust questionnaire. Answered together, they will provide the breadcrumbs to lead us back to who we truly are.

Start with people. Industrial designer Ayse Birsel takes this approach in her book *Design the Life You Love*: in one exercise, she asks that you write down your role models and the qualities you most admire about them. Then she suggests crossing out your role model's name and writing your own: the qualities identified are also yours. What can you do to express these qualities even more in your life? This is an enormously powerful exercise.

So, whom do you admire? Who were your heroes or role models ten, twenty, or thirty years ago? And, more importantly, why? What about their attitude, qualities, values, or achievements do you most admire? Perhaps one of your old bosses always seemed to find the right words to convince his team to give their best. Or you were mesmerized by your fifth-grade history teacher's ability to bring long-gone kings and generals back to life through her words. Do you perhaps admire Nelson Mandela's resilience of spirit? Or Steve Jobs's vision? Winston Churchill's eccentricity and witty eloquence?

If you cannot come up with any role models wholesale, think of specific characteristics someone possesses that inspire you. After all, nobody's perfect. Your father might have an admirable sense of fairness, even if his bad jokes make you cringe. Leslie, the CFO of a large tech company, wanted to take a few pages from her younger sister's book. Whereas Leslie had always been the poster child for duty, responsibility, and reason—not because she wanted to, but because she felt she had to—her artistic sibling exuded spontaneity, freedom, and creativity. Through coaching, Leslie gradually freed herself from feeling responsible for everyone and meeting others' expectations to the detriment of her own. She learned to say no, listen to her own desires, and be more spontaneous. By becoming better aligned with who she is, she gained energy and happiness, which, combined with her newfound creativity and better communication, also made her more efficient in her job.

Fictional characters work just as well. Who's your favorite character from a novel or movie? Perhaps you value the kind of dogged determination that fuels Sylvester Stallone's Rocky Balboa or the idealism of Robert Jordan, the hero of Ernest Hemingway's novel *For Whom the Bell Tolls*.

If people don't do it for you, period, despair not. Many roads lead to Rome. Think of colors, animals, trees, flowers, waterways, or countries. Which is your favorite? Go with the first answer that pops into your head. Then, as you

When it comes to delineating who we truly are, peripheral approaches are often far more enlightening than direct ones.

―――――――――

would with a human role models, be very specific on why. It is the significance you associate with your choices that reveals something about you, your values, and who you truly are. Do you relate to dogs' loyalty and sense of fun? Or perhaps orange is your favorite color because you find it warm and bright.

When asked about which kind of tree he would be, Sydney, one of my clients, chose the oak. Not any oak but a single oak in a meadow. Why? In his mind, he associates that image with specific qualities: the oak is solid, majestic, and solitary. To you or me, an oak might inspire entirely different associations and meaning, hence the importance of following the threads that start from our answers. One of my other clients, for example, also chose the oak, but for

———

It is the significance you associate with your choices that reveals something about you, your values, and who you truly are.

———

him the tree evokes different qualities: powerful, reassuring, productive through its many acorns, and long-lasting thanks to its deep roots.

Phillip most closely identified with a Bugatti when asked what kind of car he would be. In his mind, a Bugatti means high performance, originality, and uniqueness.

Jane picked the color green for the joy, light, and positivity it inspires for her.

You get the idea. Play with it! If these questions don't work for you, pick your favorite book or movie. Who is your favorite painter? Your favorite city? You can go the other way as well, revealing the qualities and values that matter most to you by focusing on your least favorite and working your way backwards, like a photo negative. Think of someone that triggered a *I never want to be like them!* reaction in you. Most of us only have to shake the family tree to find a few examples. For one of my clients, it was a former boss who barked at coworkers and checked his phone during meetings, which meant to my client that his boss had a fundamental lack of respect and consideration for others.

Once you gain more clarity on these fundamental qualities and values, ask yourself: do I embody these qualities and values as a person and as a leader? Are my words and actions in line with them? What can I do to align myself with these qualities and values even more?

Now that you've become more aware of the qualities and values that most matter to you, let's examine your life and what it reveals about you.

REFLECTIONS

What did you want to be as a child? Why?

_____

_____

_____

Who are your role models, real or fictitious? Why?

_____

_____

_____

If you were an animal, what would you be? Why?

_____

_____

_____

If you were a color, what would you be? Why?

_____

_____

_____

If you were a tree, what would you be? Why?

_____

_____

_____

If you were a country or a city, what would you be? Why?

_____

_____

_____

If you were a car, what would you be? Why?

_____

_____

_____

If you were a body of water, what would you be? Why?

_____

_____

_____

List all the qualities and values from your answers. How do you manifest these qualities and values as a person and as a leader?

1. _____

2. _____

3. _____

4. _____

5. _____

6. _____

7. _____

8. _____

List three steps you could take to align yourself with these qualities and values even more.

1. _____

_____

2. _____

_____

3. _____

_____

5

MAP OUT YOUR LIFE

I<small>N GALLERY</small> 825 of the Metropolitan Museum of Art in New York City hangs *Parade de cirque* by the French painter Georges Seurat, famous for his pointillism technique. The painting is made up of small dots of different colors—blue, green, orange, purple. Looked at up close, the dots seem distinct and unrelated, but if you take a few steps back, a coherent picture appears: a crowd is watching a circus sideshow at night as a mustached ringmaster looks at the trombone players.

What does a nineteenth-century painting have to do with inner alignment and leadership potential? Quite a lot, it turns out. Our lives are not much different from one of Seurat's masterpieces. Like a pointillist painting seen from up close, the thousands of events, decisions, and choices that make up our lives may at first appear separate and unrelated. Yet taken together and examined from a distance, they form a portrait. Our lives—the cards we were dealt and how we've played them—offer another rich mine of clues to who we truly are, what we value, our strengths and weaknesses, and where we want to go. The choices we've made, the opportunities we've created or seized, what we've learned—or not—have all helped shape us into who we are today. They make us unique and, as such, illuminate the kind of leader we are meant to be. There is only one problem: we are often blind to these invisible lines running through our lives. Take a few steps back, however, and seemingly unrelated elements come together to form a coherent and unique whole.

Philippe Grall's life map is a perfect illustration. On the surface, there was not much in Philippe's upbringing that heralded his calling as an executive coach in Japan. He grew up in a small village in Brittany, a world away from Asia. Yet all the seeds were there. When he was ten, karate lessons and the TV miniseries *Shōgun*—in which a lone Westerner finds himself immersed in seventeenth-century Japan—sparked a keen interest in eastern philosophies and a deep connection to Japanese rituals and values. As a teenager, Philippe's maternal grandfather encouraged his growing interest in psychology and eastern spirituality through books and conversation. Young Philippe was always keen to try out techniques such as hypnosis, first on himself and then to help others.

It took many years and a meandering journey for Philippe to realize that all these elements painted a very specific and

———

Can you identify major turning points in your life? Moments when your path veered in a different direction, due either to events beyond your control or decisions you made?

———

unique portrait of himself. He found his own alignment through trial and error, with each step bringing him closer to clarity. First was a move to Japan but for a job that was at odds with himself. Then a gradual shift towards corporate workshops via neuro-linguistic programming training—and a bank balance that was flirting with zero—eventually led him to a successful and fulfilling coaching practice. Looking back, it all makes sense. Today, his life is fully aligned with who he truly is. In other words: where he lives, what he does, and who he works with are in congruence with his values, his tastes, his talents, and the greater contribution he wants to make. The seeds were planted when he was ten, but for many years Philippe only saw disconnected dots rather than a clear picture.

To paraphrase Peter Drucker, tell me what you value, and I might believe you. But show me the twists and turns of your life and I'll show you what you really value. It is not the narratives we tell ourselves and others that are the best signposts to who we truly are, but rather it is the sum of our experiences and our actions.

Take a moment to look back. Can you identify major turning points in your life? Moments when your path veered in a different direction, due either to events beyond your control or decisions you made? Why did you make these decisions? What were your main successes and setbacks? How did you react to them? What did you learn?

A series of turning points had disrupted Wayne's early life. War had pushed his family into exile. As a young boy, he found himself a stranger in a new land, struggling to find

We are often blind to these invisible lines running through our lives.

———

his place. After his father died, he was brought up by distant relatives. Only once he took stock of his life did Wayne realize how the dislocation of his early years had shaped his values, choices, and behavior later on. As an adult, he'd consistently striven to fill the role of patriarch without being fully conscious of his behavior. At work, he'd always protected his team and taken on positions to advance social cohesion and the integration of immigrants. At home, he'd presided over a family life in which solidarity and closeness were paramount. Looking back, he was able to see clearly how important a tightly knit family and community were to him. He became aware that two of his core values were to protect those around him and cultivate close ties. Those values had shaped his professional choices and leadership style.

When faced with his next career move, that clarity made Wayne's decision about which direction to take much easier. With a greater understanding of what was important to him, he was able to make choices fully aligned with who he is.

As discussed earlier, we rarely have opportunities to stop and take stock of our own lives and make sense of them. We're often unaware of our own patterns. We tend to be blind to our talents and experience, or how we've changed over time. We don't always fully realize what drives us. It is hard to see the picture when you are in the frame. This is where the perspective of an objective outsider comes in handy, but take a crack at it yourself armed with the questions in this chapter.

Taking time to map out your life reveals enlightening patterns. When we went through this exercise together, Simone, a young entrepreneur, realized that she had repeatedly faced serious illnesses or seemingly random injuries. A close look at exact circumstances made it clear that her physical ailments had occurred whenever she felt pressured in a direction that was out of alignment with her values and purpose, but she could not find a way to make her voice heard. Unbeknownst to her, she had created physical obstacles that literally stopped her in her tracks whenever she embarked on a path that was not congruent with who she was.

I discovered a lot about myself—what I've learned and why I do what I do—by examining my own life: how I went from competitive horseback riding to advertising, entrepreneurship, and leadership coaching.[1] The decisions I made, the paths I took, the setbacks and successes I encountered have all contributed to me not only becoming an executive coach but also to the development of my own style and focus on alignment. Examining my own trajectory has illuminated what is important to me, how I want to and can contribute, and my unique identity. Understanding what I have learned from these life experiences and how they have led me to where I am has given me a strong sense of purpose that propels me in everything I do.

That kind of clarity gives you wings. So, look back at your life and unearth the map that will lead you back to yourself.

We've now used different lenses to reveal key aspects of who you are, what you value, and what drives you. In the next chapter, we'll discover what habits, beliefs, or fears might be limiting your potential.

REFLECTIONS

What are the major turning points in your life? Were these moments the result of decisions you made or events beyond your control?

_____

_____

_____

What are the most important decisions you've made? What made you choose one course of action over the others?

_____

_____

_____

What gives you energy?

_____

_____

_____

What drains your energy?

_____

_____

_____

How did you react to events beyond your control? What made you react in that way?

_____

_____

_____

_____

What have been your most triumphant successes and worst setbacks?

_____

_____

_____

_____

What are some patterns running through your life? Detail situations or decisions that seem to repeat themselves.

_____

_____

_____

_____

_____

6

IDENTIFY YOUR
SELF-LIMITATIONS

ARE YOU IN church, Hortense?"

One of my horseback riding coaches asked me that while I was preparing for the national championship at a training workshop. I looked at him dumbfounded. Church? I had no idea what he was talking about. I shook my head no.

"Then why are you praying?"

I looked down and understood what he meant. I was holding my hands very close to each other, as if in prayer position. I had been unaware of it—and of the limitation I'd been putting on myself. Once I thought about it, I remembered that, years earlier, I'd watched a famous equestrian and thought that his wide hand position was inelegant. I wanted to be a top rider but also an elegant one. In any case, it felt more natural to me to keep my hands closer to the horse's neck. Without fully realizing it, I'd been holding my hands in a position that I thought made more sense and looked better.

The trouble was that my hand position was suboptimal. Once my coach made me aware of it, it was obvious: the reins attach to the bit in the horse's mouth, and to optimize commands, the rider's hands must be far enough apart to keep the reins perfectly parallel. By adjusting my hands properly, I could "talk" to my horse far more clearly through my fingers—whose slightest movements could now be transmitted directly and accurately to the horse's mouth. Unbeknownst to me, I'd been undermining that essential line of communication, which in turn constrained my performance as a competitive show jumper.

The same happens in all areas of our lives, including in our performance as leaders. In her bestselling book, *Insight*, organizational psychologist Tasha Eurich points out that we all have blind spots about ourselves; developing self-awareness leads to more fulfillment, confidence, and success.[1] Self-limitations—often due to beliefs or fears that have turned into behavior patterns and habits—throttle our ability to stretch towards our full potential. "There is no man living who isn't capable of doing more than he thinks he can do," remarked industrialist Henry Ford.

How much do you stand in your own way, undermining your alignment?

When Robert—whom you might recall as the client from chapter 1 who constantly argued with his colleagues—first came to see me, he had been at war for years—only he didn't know it. He was respected within his company for his competence and drive, but his mistrust of others and his propensity to blow a fuse obscured his vision, weakened his standing, drained his energy, and undermined his impact. Even the words he used to describe his work life spoke of constant battle.

Does Robert's situation sound familiar? Can you think of habits or behavior of your own that might not be serving you? We all have patterns that run on loops throughout our lives like a scratched vinyl record. The same music keeps playing over and over, and the needle is not moving forward. Sometimes we can see that we're standing in our own way, but we don't know how to change. More often than not, we are not even aware of it in the first place. Why? Because our self-limitations, or hang-ups, have been with us for so long that they've become second nature. Or because they live within us for years *without* getting in our way, until we suddenly find ourselves in a situation where they do.

How can we get past our self-limitations? It starts with awareness. The first step is to shine a light on these hang-ups, so we can identify them. Just as I could not see my own misalignment when sitting in the saddle, it was difficult for Robert to see that he was trapped in constant conflict. Can you say with absolute confidence that you're fully aware of your self-limitations? Probably not. Mapping out your life (as outlined in the previous chapter) often reveals these patterns of self-limiting behavior that we all pick up along the way. A neutral observer is also much better positioned to help you identify these patterns, then unlock what hides behind them.

Where do these self-limitations come from? Our brains are constantly manufacturing meaning. Often without our conscious awareness, our brains are busy absorbing, interpreting, and connecting the stimuli that our senses collect. From in utero through the first years of life, our developing brains are like sponges: everything is absorbed at face value, stored, and combined to construct who we are. Billions of neurological pathways are created during these early years, while connections that are not needed get trimmed. All kinds of associations, fears, and beliefs get planted in our minds early on, and they strengthen over time if our thoughts routinely travel down these paths. We then lug around fears and beliefs that masquerade as immutable truths. These beliefs, often buried in our subconscious, influence our behavior like an invisible puppeteer pulling the strings. In doing so, they can limit our potential in multiple ways.

Robert first had to realize that he routinely behaved as if under attack. Once this became apparent to him, we worked on connecting the dots of his life, looking for what beliefs or fears might be hiding behind his behavior. He quickly recognized this deep-rooted siege mindset: it was borrowed from his own parents, who had survived the Second World War by being constantly on the lookout for threats that they narrowly managed to escape. By bringing this inherited mindset to light, Robert was no longer hostage to it but back in charge of his own behavior—able to decide whether being in permanent survival mode was appropriate, let alone helpful, in his current environment.

How can we get past our self-limitations? It starts with awareness.

In addition to unhelpful, outdated, or erroneous beliefs, silent fears also create self-limitations. What are you most afraid of? David's hang-up, for instance, was a fixation on money. His obsession permeated every area of his life. He was constantly checking his bank balance and putting an enormous onus on himself to bring in new business. Did he see that this was limiting his performance? Not at first. After all, aren't striving to sign new clients and keeping a close eye on the bottom line good things? Yes, they are—until they become constrictions. The pressure and angst this created for David were often self-defeating, getting in the way of his signing new clients. As we worked together and identified turning points in his life, David became aware that for years he'd been worried that he might follow in the footsteps of his father, who had gone bankrupt when David was young. Seen through his child's eyes, this had been a disaster that had erupted out of nowhere and upended his family.

Gary, my client from chapter 1 who was anxious to rush into any job after an unexpected early retirement, realized that his hang-up was related to the buried memory of a retired great-uncle, whom as a child he had perceived to be old, alone, and forgotten. He was driven by an unspoken fear that, if he stopped working even for a short while, he would become like his great-uncle. Once we connected these dots, Gary realized that he did not have to be like his relative. He then became free to imagine a different future for himself and take time to figure out what he truly wanted for the next chapter in his life.

In addition to fears, old beliefs about ourselves, fossilized into false truths that remain unchallenged, can be self-limiting. Do you find yourself saying or thinking that you're terrible at, say, drawing or singing, or perhaps that you have a great analytical mind but little imagination? I met Irene at a conference in which I was a keynote speaker. Irene's entire career had been in the nonprofit sector, and she'd become the CEO of her organization. Yet she struggled to advance her views during budget discussions with her board of directors, because she was convinced that she did not have a brain for money. What she took as a fact about her own abilities was actually a largely untested and outdated belief. Growing up in a family of engineers, she'd convinced herself that she was "bad" at math, tallying her abilities against her siblings'. She'd later extended that belief to finance without any corroborating evidence. Now that belief was limiting her potential.

There is no shortage of noise that can drown out what we truly want and turn into self-limitations. Advice from friends, family, or colleagues; expectations from parents, spouses, or mentors; peer pressure from colleagues; or notions borrowed from someone else of what success is supposed to look like. How many children have become doctors, lawyers, or soldiers not because they truly wanted to but out of family tradition or to fit their parents' idea of success? Patrick started playing soccer when he was about twelve years old. He was later selected to join a professional club to play while continuing his education at the club's middle school. By fifteen, he had signed a professional contract with a major French team. He liked it and played well; becoming a professional soccer player was a dream, but it wasn't his—it was his father's.

At age twenty-five, after Patrick had played what would be his last professional match, he decided to hang up his boots. Three months later, he was back in school. Did he ever regret his decision? No. He was too busy discovering and pursuing his own dream to spend time looking back over his father's. Patrick gave himself permission to go in another direction, and he was confident enough to see that going back to school was the right path for him. He had begun to find alignment, and he later applied what he'd learned playing soccer to a successful business career.

Self-limitations—
often due to beliefs
or fears that have
turned into behavior
patterns and
habits—throttle our
ability to stretch
towards our full
potential.

Self-limitations sometimes manifest as contradictions. Jenny, a successful entrepreneur, was ambitious and invested in her career. She was also the caring mother of two children. When I first met her, Jenny was entangled in an endless court battle with business partners. Although she was determined to keep progressing in her career, one thing after another conspired against her. While she was clear about her own values as a working mother, she came to realize that her own mother's vocal disapproval of her working had been weighing on her. Her mother's voice had lodged itself in her psyche, creating inner friction of which Jenny was not initially aware. She was trapped between her own values and her mother's, and this misalignment was resulting in conflicting actions that held her back. Identifying it gave her the freedom to disentangle herself from beliefs that were not congruent with who she was and what she wanted.

Are you able to identify all your self-limitations? Difficult, isn't it? You're not alone. Again, unless someone is holding up a mirror, we often fail to see when what we think and what we say are at odds with what we do. You may think (and say) that you value your family, but do you give your spouse and children your undivided attention when you spend time with them? Or do you keep checking your phone and strategizing about your next board meeting?

Adding to the challenge, what holds you back today might be the very same thing that had served you well in the past. Marshall Goldsmith titled one of his books *What Got You Here Won't Get You There* after this very reality. I've worked with many clients whose careers had been built on their technical expertise and who were used to being recognized and rewarded for their knowledge, not for their ability to inspire and coach their team. More senior leadership positions required letting go of what had been the source of their success. Hanging on to modes of operation that worked well in different circumstances became an obstacle for them.

Can you identify beliefs and patterns that no longer serve you? What behavior or thoughts would you most like to shift? What, or whom, do they remind you of? Can you trace them back to their source? When you become aware of your source(s) of conflict, you gain the freedom to let go of behaviors and beliefs that limit your evolution. You open a door, and you have a choice to make. Once I became aware that my hand position was undermining my riding, I had to choose between appearance and performance. I chose performance.

Now that you're clearer about who you are and have identified the self-limitations that you're ready to ditch, what steps can you take to bring about and maintain a better inner alignment? Read on.

REFLECTIONS

What behavior patterns would you like to change?

_____

_____

Of whom or what do they remind you?

_____

_____

_____

What is your worst fear? Where does it come from?

_____

_____

_____

What are your beliefs? What proof confirms that they are true?

_____

_____

_____

What do you want to get better at?

_____

_____

PART TWO

Meet Your Potential

"Finding alignment is not about becoming someone else. It is about connecting with the best version of the leader that already exists within you."

_____

THE STORY GOES that Michelangelo was once asked how he sculpted his statue of David. "The sculpture is already complete within the marble block before I start my work," the Renaissance master is said to have replied. "I just have to chisel away the superfluous material."

You are that masterpiece within the marble block. All you can be already lives within you, waiting to be unleashed and realized. Finding alignment is not about becoming someone else. It is about connecting with the best version of the leader that already exists within you and bringing it forth by chiseling away all that obscures and restrains it.

Part I of this book was about delineating the masterpiece. You should now have a clearer view of who you truly are: your values and strengths, the larger purpose that drives you, how your life has shaped you, and the self-limitations that might stand in your way.

Part II is about removing the superfluous material—the self-limitations, distractions, and other noise that drain your energy, perspective, and clarity—so you can progress towards inner alignment and enhance your potential as a leader. First, we'll explore how you can rewire your brain to transcend the self-limitations you identified in Part I. Next, we'll address how you can enhance your energy, sense of ease, and overall alignment by cultivating positive emotions and shifting your perspective, particularly when it comes to failure. Then we'll move on to the role of intuition in alignment, how you can cultivate that intuition and stay connected with, and focused on, what you really want and your sense of purpose. Finally, we'll discuss how to bridge your inner alignment with your environment.

7

REWIRE YOUR BRAIN

NOW THAT YOU'RE aware of your self-limitations and have decided to let go of what is keeping you from moving forward, what's next? How do you move past your hang-ups? By retraining your brain.

I had a close connection to Hermione, the horse with whom I competed as a teenager. I could read her moods, and she seemed to understand mine. We trained well together, learning to communicate better and be in sync with each other. Working with her, however, I quickly realized that my mare had a major hang-up: she was terrified of water. Every time Hermione saw a river or a stream, she stalled and refused to jump. I tried to distract her so she wouldn't spot the obstacle in advance, but this didn't work very well. I have no idea how she had developed her phobia; I can only guess that she had been hurt in a context that involved water. Her brain clearly associated it with danger, which dictated her behavior and limited her potential.

If we were to compete together, we would have to tackle her fear, so we got to work. I would take her to a river and walk next to her, holding her bridle and talking softly. I had her drink from my hand. We went to the beach together, and I gently wet her face. We did this for months; little by little, she came to associate water with joy rather than terror. Eventually, she became entirely comfortable jumping over water obstacles. Her brain had been rewired.

For centuries, scientists believed that once we reached adulthood, our brains were immutable. This has now been debunked. Fortunately for us, researchers have figured out that our brains are in fact able to change throughout our lives—something known as neuroplasticity. Neurons are able to develop new connections, and synapses can weaken or strengthen over time. It turns out that our brains even seem able to transfer functions from one region to another. This extraordinary ability can give us enormous power.

In his book *The Brain That Changes Itself*, psychiatrist Norman Doidge shares the case of Catalan poet and scholar Pedro Bach-y-Rita, who in 1959 suffered a disabling stroke that paralyzed his face and half of his body, leaving him unable to speak. His son, who was told there was no hope of recovery, decided that he would approach his father's motor rehabilitation the same way we learn as babies. Instead of trying to have his father walk, he would first teach him to crawl. It was a struggle at first, but after a few months, Bach-y-Rita could walk on all fours. Practicing several hours a day,

By rewiring your brain, you have the power to replace limiting beliefs with more supportive ones.

---

he then went from crawling to standing, and from standing to walking. He learned how to speak and write again and eventually went back to full-time teaching. During his spare time, he traveled, hiked, and climbed, living a full life.

Seven years later, Bach-y-Rita died of a heart attack at age seventy-two. An autopsy revealed that the massive damage from his stroke had never healed. The major brain centers that control movement, as well as most of his brain stem, were completely shattered. In fact, 97 per cent of the nerves that linked his cerebral cortex to his spine had been destroyed, which had resulted in his initial paralysis. How had he been able to recover most of his functions in spite of such devastating damage? Hours of rehabilitation and training had stimulated the brain to reorganize itself, creating new connections that compensated for the lesions and resulted in his remarkable recovery. Bach-y-Rita's brain had rewired itself, creating back roads that bypassed the destroyed neural highways.

What does neural rewiring after a stroke have to do with moving past your self-limitations? The same neural reconditioning is possible with habits and behaviors. Once I became aware that my hands were not positioned effectively while riding, and then decided to let go of this unhelpful habit, I began to consciously focus on keeping my hands further apart every time I was in the saddle. Eventually, this hand position took root as a new, positive habit, so I no longer had to think about it. My riding skills improved markedly, and I unlocked potential I did not know I had.

The same can be said of beliefs. Think of them like muscles. If you've been running all your life, your legs will be in good shape, but your arms might be on the weak side. One day you decide that you'd like to develop upper-body strength. What can you do? You can start doing push-ups. If you do them every day, your muscles gradually grow stronger. Just as you can develop killer biceps by exercising those specific muscles, you can train your brain by creating new neural connections. By rewiring your brain, you have the power to replace limiting beliefs with more supportive ones. This is like upgrading your own operating system: changing your beliefs allows you to change your behavior and your outcomes.

Your brain produces an average of about 50,000 thoughts every single day. Most of the time, you're not aware of them. Most are repetitive and automatic—little more than background noise. They partly reflect the neural connections that have developed over your life. But through these thoughts you can either reinforce the neural highways already there or create and strengthen new paths.

Once you've worked through Part I of this book—you've pulled your hang-ups out of the shadows of your subconscious and decided to let go of them—you're already halfway there. Replacing these hang-ups with new associations and habits that will help unlock hidden potential takes attention and practice: think of it as push-ups for your brain. Focus on the self-limitation you've decided to change. Pay attention and practice. Every day, ask yourself, "Did I do my best today to focus on this and behave differently?" This is what Marshall Goldsmith refers to as a "daily question."

After we started working together, Harriet, a senior vice-president at a food manufacturing company, realized she took a dim view of financial success. She'd been raised to believe that money made people selfish and arrogant. She had plenty of examples to reinforce her views, which she therefore held as absolute truth. Consequently, she felt that any raise she might receive would tarnish her character.

After Harriet became fully aware of what money meant to her, we worked on deciding whether or not her belief was indeed true. Was everyone with money selfish or arrogant? Of course not. Could she make a different choice if she were to earn more money? Yes, she could. How would she spend money if she had more of it? She decided that she would buy a family house, where children and grandchildren could all gather together. We worked on strengthening this new, far more positive association. Rather than seeing money as corrupting character, it became a tool for bringing her loved ones closer, which was important to her. By extension, this meant that working towards making more money was no longer despicable but a very worthy objective.

Next, Harriet strengthened that new neural wiring through sustained attention and repetition. Every day, she asked herself, "Did I do my best to work towards my family house today?" She thought of actions she could take, including looking for a house, and she found one. This gave her the drive to ask for a substantial raise—which she obtained. Her earnings further increased when she was given more responsibilities. Becoming aware of the negative connotations that she had been associating with money gave her the freedom to sever that link and replace it with a clear and positive purpose. By shifting away from old, limiting beliefs and rewiring her brain to align with new, more supportive ones, Harriet was able to unlock a fuller expression of her true self.

What new connections and behaviors can replace the old beliefs that no longer serve you? Which positive associations would you like to create? Which one or two will you focus on first?

Keep noticing, practicing, and doing your best. Every day! Listen to the voice that, like *Pinocchio*'s Jiminy Cricket, keeps you focused on positive beliefs and behaviors until they take root and become your new normal.

The next few chapters will examine how rewiring your brain can further support your inner alignment when applied to several critical areas: emotions, setbacks, and intuition.

———

What new connections and behaviors can replace the old beliefs that no longer serve you? Which positive associations would you like to create?

———

REFLECTIONS

Which self-limitations are you ready to move past?

_____

_____

_____

_____

List one or two you would like to focus on first.

_____

_____

_____

_____

What would happen if you let go of these self-limitations?
Give one answer for each.

_____

_____

_____

_____

Are you willing to let those "what would happen" scenarios unfold?

_____

_____

_____

_____

Write a daily question to remind yourself of your decision, and practice—every day.

_____

_____

_____

_____

8

THE POWER OF
POSITIVE EMOTIONS

GROWING UP, I used to exercise with a friend. Our form of exercise was a bit particular, however: we practiced laughing. Whether something was funny or not. Whenever we couldn't find an obvious reason to crack up, we'd force ourselves to laugh like demented hyenas. And regardless of how we started laughing, our practice always ended the same way: we brought ourselves to stitches, tears rolling down our cheeks as we roared hysterically. The act of laughing, even when initially forced, always became authentic.

Seeing each other laugh was contagious. Without knowing it, we were experiencing the power of mirror neurons—and also becoming experts at cultivating positive emotions.

Some neurons have been found to fire not only when we perform an action or go through an emotion but also when we observe others going through it. This helps explain why we are influenced by the mood and actions of people around us. This means that emotions, as I first found out laughing with my friend, affect more than the person who feels them.

Would you like to be more productive, creative, resilient, and energetic? What about becoming better at spotting opportunities and creatively solving complex problems? Would you say that cranking up the volume on these qualities would give you a significant edge? Neurological research has confirmed that when you adopt a positive mood and outlook, your brain is able to produce a broader range of thoughts and ideas, as well as store and retrieve information faster and more productively. A positive brain also makes more neural connections, which means faster, more creative thinking and problem-solving. In other words, your brain—thanks to the release of dopamine and serotonin triggered by positive emotions—is more productive, creative, resilient, and energetic. How about that for an edge?

This is what Shawn Achor, a leading expert on human potential, has labeled "the happiness advantage," which he compares to Copernicus's discovery that the sun does not revolve around the Earth. It is not success that fuels happiness (defined as the experience of positive emotions, incorporating deeper feelings of meaning and purpose): it is happiness that facilitates success.[1]

This concept extends to aligned leadership. Cultivating positive emotions facilitates a sense of inner alignment by easing friction and energy drain. In *Power vs. Force,*

Cultivating positive emotions facilitates a sense of inner alignment by easing friction and energy drain.

———

psychiatrist David Hawkins (first discussed in chapter 1) ranks emotions based on how they impact our life and our power. Hawkins's concept means that effective leadership radiates power and does not rely on force—think of Mahatma Gandhi or the Dalai Lama. So, how do we boost our power? Hawkins argues that positive emotions such as serenity, bliss, optimism, forgiveness, or gratitude enhance our power. Feelings such as shame, guilt, fear, anger, or regret diminish it.[2]

Cultivating positive emotions therefore becomes an essential element of effective leadership. When you project these emotions, you set the tone around you and model a positive attitude for your team. Sigal Barsade of the Wharton School has studied how leaders' emotions shape the feelings of people around them—a phenomenon known as "emotional contagion." Focusing on the positive in all situations and all people also helps to resolve complicated situations more quickly. When I co-created and led an R&D company in steel recycling, staying optimistic kept me, my business partner, and our research team motivated when we encountered setbacks and felt discouraged. A positive attitude gave us hope, energy, and confidence. We were able to come up with the next idea and invariably find solutions to tricky chemical challenges. Maintaining a positive outlook at the top helped maintain an innovative atmosphere and mindset throughout the company.

It can be easier said than done, of course. How can you be happy when life throws you a nasty curveball? And what if patience is not your forte, and you tend to easily get angry or irritated? Maybe it is far easier for you to imagine what could go wrong, rather than what could go right. Isn't this part of your innate personality, an immutable part of who you are?

It doesn't have to be. Remember the push-ups for your brain? Positivity, like everything else, takes practice—just as building muscles requires exercise. Thoughts trigger emotions. By consciously shifting your thoughts, you have the power to alter your emotions.

"I pray and laugh a lot," says Jennifer Paylor, the head of the coaching practice at IBM, when asked how she keeps a healthy sense of perspective. "When you start to forget about God, family, fun, praying, your values, and your purpose in this world, then you need to rethink your own alignment."

There are many tools to help you. Here are a few I like to use. Remember specific moments that brought you joy or happiness. Visualize where you were and what happened. Your brain does not differentiate between visualization and reality: imagining that you're lifting your hand, for example, stimulates the same parts of your brain that would be stimulated if you were actually doing it. By visualizing a time associated with positive emotions, you have the power to activate these emotions again. This is a powerful antidote if you feel yourself drifting towards irritability, frustration, or blame.

Take Rose, the head of marketing in a retail company. Extremely conscientious, she was serious to a fault. She found it challenging to experience joy beyond fleeting moments. She didn't smile much, let alone laugh. She was not unhappy, but she lacked any sense of lightheartedness, which wasn't much fun for Rose or those around her. Her lackluster outlook set the tone, and the atmosphere at the office left little space for joy. She struggled to inject positivity into her attitude, particularly when confronted with setbacks.

We worked on constructing a bank of visualizations that she could tap into whenever needed. I asked her to remember a moment of unadulterated happiness and to bring herself back to that moment. She had to see it and feel it. Rose was silent for a moment, thinking. "I watched my daughter jump with both feet into puddles the other day," she said. "She was laughing, splashing water. That filled me with joy." Once Rose deposited that moment into her memory bank, she was able to fill with joy whenever and

———

Feed your own power by adopting a positive attitude. Focus on what you can change and impact, and find a way around everything else.

———

wherever she wanted: all she had to do was to visualize her daughter jumping in puddles, which immediately brought a smile to her face.

In addition to visualization, shifting perspectives is a good practice that cultivates inner alignment through positive emotions. Imagine looking at a landscape with grey- and then yellow-tinted glasses. You will see the identical landscape in entirely different lights: in one case, drab and dull; in the other, warm and vibrant. Same setting, entirely different experience. The same is true of every situation. Think of a movie or a book. Have you noticed how you remember different details and may even come up with a different interpretation than someone else? You watched or read in light of your own mindset and past experience, which influences how the book or movie resonates with you. Your interpretation of events or conversations determine the meaning you assign to them, and that meaning determines how you feel about them. But you have the power to shift your perspective. Can you find silver linings instead of focusing on what goes wrong? When you find that your thoughts are dwelling on a litany of challenges, can you instead think of what is going well in your life? Feed your own power by adopting a positive attitude. Focus on what you can change and impact, and find a way around everything else.

Whatever happens, keep smiling—even just a little. It might feel forced at first, but just as my childhood friend and I always ended up laughing hysterically after initially pretending, your smile will help you. Why? The physical act of smiling sends positive signals to your brain and instantly tricks it into shifting gears towards more positive emotions. Try it! Just smile, for no particular reason, and pay attention. What happens? Do you notice a slight inner shift?

Make training your brain this way part of your daily routine, like brushing your teeth. Do at least one thing that gives you joy, however small: listen to your favorite song, call your favorite person, walk around the block, or take five minutes for a coffee. Can you find ways to laugh at least twice a day? Create your own bank of positive moments by visualizing instances when you felt intense joy, and bring them back to mind whenever you feel like you need an uplifting breath. And keep asking yourself: did I do my best to experience moments of joy, gratitude, and happiness today?

Cultivating positive emotions brings a shift in perspective that helps chip away the "superfluous material" obscuring your inner alignment. The ability to shift perspective towards a more positive outlook is particularly crucial when dealing with failure, the topic of the next chapter.

REFLECTIONS

How many times did you laugh today?

_____

Do you tend to see the glass half-full or half-empty?

_____

Remember specific moments of unadulterated positive emotion (joy, happiness, gratitude, hysterical laughter, etc.). Where were you? With whom? What were the circumstances? Reconnect with these moments, and write them down. What do you feel?

_____

_____

_____

_____

_____

Smile. What does it feel like? Do you notice an inner shift?

_____

_____

9

THE GIFT OF "FAILURE"

HOW COMFORTABLE ARE you with failure? Horseback riding taught me valuable lessons about that F word. First, one must fall at least a hundred times to be considered a good equestrian—and the more one falls, the less intimidating and dreaded it becomes. Second, failure is a very effective teacher, and there is always more to learn. If I did well in a race, I took time to celebrate before quickly focusing on how I could improve and do even better going forward. Yet when I did poorly, it offered the chance to learn even more. What mistakes had I made and how could I correct them? Third, I learned that the horse is never to blame when things go wrong; only the rider is.

These lessons served me well when I decided to start my own business. My first business idea was to leverage both my knowledge of horses and experience in marketing and communication by creating a polo team that would be sponsored by a large company. This seemed perfectly aligned with who I was. I loved the project, on which I worked for nine months before realizing that the timing was not right: firms were not ready to invest much in sponsorship while the economy was lukewarm. But I did not want to give up on my dream of creating my own company. I decided that if my first idea didn't work, another one would. In fact, that initial attempt carried the seeds of the business I would later create. While researching the polo team idea, I met an industrial entrepreneur who worked with raw material. He introduced me to a world I knew nothing about, and together we started our business in the steel recycling industry.

Had I not rebounded after my first setback and kept an open mind, this opportunity would have passed me by, as this was not something I could have imagined in a million years. But the entrepreneur was the right person, and our venture was the right idea in the right environment at the right moment. It also turned out to be the right business for me: one out of my comfort zone which helped me grow, learn, and evolve. Was it always easy? Of course not. Once the company was up and running, we had to navigate multiple setbacks; the French bureaucracy put countless obstacles in our way; we had to change strategies several times; and our research did not pan out the way we hoped for at first. But we eventually developed an innovative technology and found the right home for it. Along the way, I learned a lot not only about the industry but also about leading people.

If you don't want
to fail, chances are
you won't take risks
either—and without
meaningful risks,
you're unlikely to
innovate or soar.

The journey towards alignment requires exploration, and exploration is not a straight road. There are sometimes dead-ends and meandering routes. To lead well, you must learn to deal with failure productively, which might require a shift in perspective. Start with yourself. Effective leadership requires the openness to keep learning and the resilience to keep trying when confronted with inevitable setbacks. Why? Because the world around us changes. As technology and globalization disrupt products, services, and traditional ways of doing business, you must adapt and anticipate to succeed. Staying in your comfort zone leads to complacency. Constantly learning to do and be better, and being willing to try new things, on the other hand, fuels your growth as a leader and, by extension, the growth of those around you. To evolve, you have to take risks. Sometimes they pay off. And when they don't, you're given a chance to learn.

"I have not failed," Thomas Edison is rumored to have said when asked about his experiments to develop the incandescent light bulb. "I have just found 10,000 ways that won't work." To the great inventor, that which did not work was only feedback that brought him closer to what would. Or ask James Dyson, who spent fifteen years working on more than 5,000 versions of his bagless vacuum cleaner before he made one that worked.

Psychologist and innovation researcher Samuel West is a firm believer in the lessons of failure. He was so tired of hearing and reading the "same boring success stories" that he created and now curates the Museum of Failure, a collection of failed products and services from around the world, based in Sweden. The museum includes jewels such as Bic for Her, purple and pink glitter ball pens for women launched in 2011 at double the price of regular pens. Or Coca-Cola BläK, a combination of soda and coffee launched in 2006—and discontinued in 2008. Pringle Olestra, anyone? In 1996, consumers were treated with this fat-free crisp. The catch? It gave them diarrhea and stomach cramps. "It is in the failures we find the interesting stories we can learn from," West explains. To help spread the message, the museum has spawned a pop-up version—showcasing failures in innovation, healthcare, and finance—traveling around the world.[1]

Setbacks become failures only if you stop trying or get paralyzed ruminating on what has not worked. During a race, a rider cannot afford to mull endlessly over the obstacle that that has gone wrong. Instead, she must focus on the obstacle ahead. This is a mindset that my great-grandfather and role model Ernest fully internalized while breeding a draft horse known as Boulonnais in northern France. For the 1910 Centennial International Exposition in Buenos Aires, Argentina invited other countries to showcase draft horses; back then the South American country bred mainly polo horses. Convinced that the Boulonnais was the best draft horse, Ernest saw an opportunity and petitioned the French ministry of agriculture to present his breed at the exposition. He was turned down, and the government decided to showcase another breed, the Percheron, instead. Furious and frustrated, Ernest was nonetheless undeterred.

He approached other Boulonnais breeders and convinced them one by one to join forces and go to Argentina anyway. He then arranged a boat to transport 150 horses across the Atlantic. The financial risk could have turned into a disaster, but once in Argentina, Ernest was vindicated: the Boulonnais breed became a sensation. Subsequently, Ernest successfully exported Boulonnais to Argentina, where he traveled annually.

Embracing failure is not easy, however. Nobody likes to fall flat on their face. Even if we understand the value in setbacks, it is natural to feel disappointed, frustrated, embarrassed, and discouraged when things don't work out. Setbacks can dent self-confidence and breed doubt, which in turns breeds risk aversion. "Am I inadequate? What if the next attempt does not succeed either?"

How do you instead build the ability to move past the initial disappointment, learn from setbacks, stretch yourself, and keep going? This is where alignment and some brain rewiring come in. The energy that comes from the connection to oneself and others, the clear sense of purpose, the ease and calm: all feed that willingness and ability to stretch, the ability to uncover silver linings and fresh ideas, and the resilience to keep going in spite of setbacks. That's what happens when what you set out to do feeds your sense of purpose.

Aicha Evans's spectacular career at the Intel Corporation was not without spectacular failures.[2] After pitching a new product line of smartphone and tablet chips known as SoFIA to the executive team, Evans obtained the full backing and

For leaders, dealing with setbacks productively also means accepting responsibility.

---

funding from Intel, which had been struggling to establish itself in the mobile market. As she drove the project, however, Evans and her team ran into technical issues that they were not able to solve. Two years later, the project had to be dropped. This was a very public failure for Evans, with the board and the media well aware of the project and its outcome.

Evans is frank about how hard it was at first to admit defeat and then digest such a spectacular setback. But she got over her initial anger and disappointment and looked for the silver lining. She was then able to focus on what had gone wrong and what lessons could be learned from it—for both herself and the company. First, she realized that she had not sufficiently looked at Intel's earlier attempts to develop similar products and why they had failed, which could have informed her own efforts. Besides the personal lesson, this process allowed her to identify and flag fundamental gaps that affected other Intel products. This gave Intel the opportunity to tackle these shortcomings, with benefits that were felt across other product lines.

Just as alignment gave Evans the resilience to leverage her setback, losing it led Gregory Renard to a sense of failure. Cofounder and chief artificial intelligence officer at xBrain, Renard gradually lost his bearings after moving from France to Silicon Valley. The move made sense, as AI prospects in France appeared limited. Once in California, however, Renard started working on projects he did not believe in, such as AI applications in cars. Within three years, Gregory hit rock bottom. "Whatever I do," he realized, "I'm in failure mode." He decided to change course. Using the same technology, he pivoted from cars to customer service, which was far better aligned with his sense of purpose: he developed a platform to create, set up, and manage AI customer service agents for clients. This enabled 24/7 customer support and freed up call center employees from repetitive tasks. Far from that sense of failure, Gregory has rebounded to a successful and profitable path.

For leaders, dealing with setbacks productively also means accepting responsibility. Just as aligned equestrians never blame their horse, aligned leaders own failures—their collaborators' as well as their own. Following the principle of emotional contagion (discussed in the previous chapter), your attitude towards failure influences your team's. Aicha Evans explains that when she decided to take full and sole responsibility for the SoFIA failure, two things happened. First, it eased the anxiety of her team members, who were worried about the consequences of the project's implosion. It also signaled to them that she too could fail, and that failing was okay and could result in worthy learnings.

Armed with the knowledge that you can rewire your brain, adopt a "growth mindset" for yourself and others. Stanford University psychologist Carol Dweck has famously argued that cultivating a growth mindset—the belief that talents and abilities are not fixed but instead can be developed—fosters outstanding accomplishments. It encourages perpetual learning, with setbacks seen as opportunities to improve. Executive coaching is based on this premise of perpetual growth potential. On the other hand, people or organizations with a "fixed mindset" believe in innate intelligence and talents. They are less likely to flourish, because they avoid failure at all costs.[3] If you don't want to fail, chances are you won't take risks either—and without meaningful risks, you're unlikely to innovate or soar.

Think of your biggest setbacks. How did you respond to them? What have you learned from them? Have you embraced learning and moved on? Do you have a growth mindset or a fixed mindset?

In the next few chapters, we'll explore additional tools to help you keep carving out that superfluous material and better align yourself.

REFLECTIONS

How did you respond to your biggest setbacks, and what made you react that way?

_____

_____

_____

_____

What lessons have you learned from your setbacks?

_____

_____

_____

_____

Do you have a growth mindset or a fixed mindset?

_____

_____

_____

_____

10

VALUE YOUR INTUITION

Hᴏᴡ ᴅᴏ ʏᴏᴜ know that you're making the right decision? What is that little voice in your head telling you to do (or not do)? How important is that voice in your journey towards better alignment?

Ross had a successful career at a top management consulting firm when one of his clients, a major technology company, offered him a senior executive position. Ross had a choice to make. He could stay in his existing consulting job, in which he excelled and was generously remunerated. Or he could follow a riskier but more exciting path, putting into practice the strategic advice that he had been devising, leading a large team, and gaining operational experience. Was this the path he really wanted to follow, and if so, was it the right moment to jump ship? Or should he stay in his comfortable and familiar position? Ross carefully weighed the multiple pros and cons of each option, but flexing his analytical muscle alone did not yield any obvious answer. A friend suggested he ditch his list of pluses and minuses. "What does your gut tell you?" his friend asked. Ross immediately knew the answer. He would accept the job offer. A part of his mind knew that this was the best course of action for him. And indeed it was: Ross flourished, both professionally and personally, in his new role, which opened the door to an even more successful career and led him to become the CEO of several large companies.

That "sensing" is intuition: the ability to know directly and immediately without conscious reasoning or inference. Have you ever experienced a moment of unexplained insight? A gut feeling? An inner voice? A deep conviction that just feels right? Perhaps a sneaky feeling that you should take your umbrella with you even though the sun is shining, and sure enough it rains. A surprising clarity on exactly what decision to make, even though you don't have perfect information or time to weigh the pros and cons. The conviction that you've just met the person you will marry. Or an ability to pick up on what is not being said, like someone else's unease or a tense interaction. This is your intuition speaking to you.

Albert Einstein referred to the intuitive mind as "a sacred gift" and the rational mind as "a faithful servant." He remarked, "We have created a society that honors the servant and has forgotten the gift." Formal education indeed puts enormous emphasis on cultivating reasoning and analytical abilities. We're groomed to trust data, analysis, and hard proof. As a result, we come to disregard our intuition, or at least to relegate it to a back seat.

Yet leaders have to rely on intuition to make better, more aligned decisions when facing complicated choices. Why? Because analysis and reason, while highly useful, have their own limitations. They rely on existing knowledge, linear processes, and what can be measured. The future, however, is made of that which we cannot yet be certain. Information is imperfect and incomplete—or overwhelming. Intuition, on the other hand, is about lightning speed, lateral connections, and complexity, which turn out to be very useful when making complicated decisions.

First, speed. Rational, linear, and conscious reasoning has been shown to be far slower than intuition. In prehistoric times, intuition and instinct were essential to our survival. Escaping saber-tooth tigers required a sixth sense for danger and speedy decisions. There was no time to collect data, analyze, or consider pros and cons, which is what our prefrontal cortex does. This is why our rational selves often cannot at first make sense of our intuitive insights, which often then get discarded.

But our intuition often "feels" the answer before our rational selves can work their way to the same conclusion. In a study simulating real-life decisions in a context of uncertainty, rewards, and penalties, players were given four decks of cards, a $2,000 loan, and instructions to play to win the most money. Players had no idea that the decks had been constructed to result in very different overall gains and losses.

After suffering a few large losses from the "bad" decks, the players' palms started to sweat ever so slightly—a reaction caused by the primitive fight, flight, or freeze response to danger—whenever they considered picking from these decks. This suggested that, although the players were unaware of it, they intuitively knew which decks were riskier. They had to keep playing much longer, however, before they reported having a hunch about which were the riskier decks, and even longer before they could explain why the two "bad" decks should be avoided. Even the few players who never consciously figured it out still instinctively avoided the disadvantageous decks.[1]

Now, complexity. Conventional wisdom favors careful, conscious deliberation when making important decisions, but in complex situations, conscious deliberation often leads to poor decisions. Our conscious mind can process a far more limited amount of information than our intuitive mind. Furthermore, our conscious reasoning turns out to be rather poor at correctly weighing various factors that it takes into consideration. In other words, the importance of some considerations gets overinflated, while others get inaccurately minimized. This produces a misalignment, resulting in decisions that we come to regret or that do not quite match our priorities and values. Scientific experiments have confirmed that while conscious deliberation produces better outcomes for simple choices, complex decisions involving multiple factors are better served by subconscious deliberation while one's attention is directed elsewhere—taking a mental step back and letting the intuitive mind do the heavy lifting.[2]

Our conscious mind can process a far more limited amount of information than our intuitive mind.

I have relied on intuition throughout my life. As a teenager, I decided to spend several summers in the United States. On the face of it, this made no sense. In France, summertime is the height of the show jumping season, for which I still trained relentlessly. But my intuition kept telling me, "Go West, young woman!" Before I was even aware of it, I sensed I was getting ready for a new chapter in my life. I found a landing spot for the summer with a stable owner who had fifteen horses. Several years later, that experience convinced me to choose a university program that included one year in an American college—now commonplace in many French universities but back then unheard of. This ended up changing the course of my life. I felt at home in the open-minded, dynamic, and entrepreneurial culture of the United States, which broadened my outlook on life and armed me with an unshakable sense of optimism. Had I made my initial decision by consciously weighing the pros and cons of each option, I probably would have gone around in circles and not spent the summer in the United States.

Speed and complexity are two essential elements with which today's and tomorrow's leaders have to contend. In this context, leaders able to tap into their intuition have a significant advantage. No wonder some Silicon Valley executives and elite military teams have been pushing the envelope, exploring how to access and harness altered states of consciousness to unlock insights, unleash high performance, and solve critical challenges.[3]

Intuition also feeds into emotional intelligence, also known as EQ, which, alongside the ability to make decisions, is an essential leadership quality. Developed by Daniel Goleman, this concept refers to "a set of skills, including control of one's impulses, self-motivation, empathy, and social competence in interpersonal relationships."[4] A very successful CEO told me that he wished he'd known much earlier in his career that when it comes to leadership, EQ is far more important than IQ. The ability to recognize and process one's emotions, as well as others', taps more into your intuitive abilities than your analytical ones. Within a fraction of a second, your brain is able to read thousands of micro expressions in someone else's face, body language, or even mood without being aware of it.

Chris, a tech entrepreneur, was about to sign a very important deal. Two days before closing it, he intuitively sensed that his client was getting cold feet and being evasive. Chris immediately adjusted his stance: instead of pressing his client as he had initially intended, he sensed that he should ask questions and listen to his client's concerns. In doing so, he realized his client was scared. The stock market had softened over the summer, and doubt over the deal had crept in. Panicked, the client wanted to put everything on hold. Chris was able to connect and convince him that the market turmoil was temporary, and to move forward on the deal would send reassuring signals to his investors and collaborators. His client mulled over it for a few days and decided to sign the deal.

Because intuition is better connected to speed, complexity, and emotional intelligence, systematically favoring our rational over our intuitive selves when making complicated decisions often leads to misalignment. Take what happened to Karen when she considered two different job offers. She connected well with everyone she met from the first company throughout the interview process. The job was interesting, and the corporate culture felt like a good fit. The second job offer, however, was far more prestigious, with enticing career prospects and a more central location. Karen enjoyed being congratulated for receiving the second job offer, while the first one did not generate the same admiration. Karen carefully considered the pros and cons of each, but she ignored the voice inside her that kept telling her she was far more comfortable with the first company. She accepted the second offer.

From day one, Karen's prestigious new job felt wrong. She enjoyed neither the work or the management style. She was a fish out of water among her new colleagues, whose values and priorities did not feel aligned with hers. She kept telling herself to give it time, but she dreaded going to the office. After six months, Karen was clinically depressed, suffering from an array of psychosomatic ailments and barely able to drag herself out of bed in the morning. Unlike Ross, who had relied on his intuition to make a decision that aligned with who he was, Karen was paying the price for refusing to acknowledge that her rational decision had left her in drastic misalignment with herself. The moment Karen decided to quit, an enormous weight was lifted from her shoulders. Listening to her intuition, she decided to reorient her career in a direction far more in line with what she truly wanted to do.

I am not advocating that you ignore your analytical, rational mind. Slower but far more nuanced, precise, and sophisticated, it houses memories and values, and it is much better able to follow rules. Exploring and embracing complexity, considering different angles, and collecting data before relying on intuition for a decision helps to avoid oversimplifications.[5]

We need both our analytical and intuitive minds. My suggestion is that you balance the scales between the lightning-fast, profound, and creative insights that can come only from your intuition and the higher functions of your conscious intelligence. Recognize when your intuition is speaking to you, and listen. Leaders able to rely on both analytics and intuition make better, more aligned decisions, and they are far more agile in the face of change.

———

"Sensing" is intuition: the ability to know directly and immediately without conscious reasoning or inference.

———

They are also more attuned to apparent coincidences and "luck." Napoleon used to ask military officers if they were lucky before promoting them. What he wanted to know was whether they listened to their intuition and were therefore able to spot and seize opportunities in the moment—much like he did himself. Napoleon prepared his battles carefully, studying the terrain and his opponents' tactics, yet he knew when to rely on his intuition, which made him a formidable adversary.[6]

How much do you rely on your intuition when making decisions? Do you trust it? Are you able to tap into it, setting aside your conscious deliberation when you want to? The more you become aware of your intuition and learn to trust it, the more it has a chance to develop. Think of it as another form of brain rewiring, and flex these neural pathways.

Now that we've clarified the role of intuition in making better aligned decisions, the next chapter provides tools to reclaim some mindspace.

REFLECTIONS

How much do you rely on your intuition when making decisions? Think of instances when you made decisions that did not seem rational but felt right.

_____

_____

_____

_____

How much do you trust your intuition?

_____

_____

What do you do to "switch off" your analytical mind when you want to?

_____

_____

_____

_____

_____

11

RECLAIM SOME MINDSPACE

HOW CAN YOU cultivate inner alignment amidst all the noise in your life?

Bill never stopped. The CEO of a financial services company, he went from meeting to meeting, from plane to plane. His schedule was full. His head was full. Mind racing, he came up with idea after idea, never stopping to consider which might be worth pursuing and dropping initiatives as quickly as he started them. Always rushing, he acted before considering what was most important or when action was needed at all. Convinced that he knew what his collaborators meant to say before they even finished their sentences, he kept interrupting everyone to speed things up. Amid all that inner noise and agitation, he had lost touch with himself and with his intuition. As we worked together, Bill first realized that his hyperactivity was limiting his effectiveness and decided he wanted to reconnect with a quieter part of himself. But how?

Have you ever felt that your brain is suffering from information overload? Or that your thoughts go around and around in a loop, like a hamster stuck on its wheel? How can you hear your aligned self amid the 50,000 or so thoughts that vie for your headspace every day? Thoughts about the meeting that happened yesterday, or next week's business trip. Thoughts about what one of your colleagues said, or how you will present your new strategy to the board. Complex decisions to make, sifting through a deluge of conflicting views and data. Balancing short-term considerations and long-term strategic imperatives, or the interests of the board, shareholders, business partners, and employees.

To make room for your intuition and stay connected with your aligned self, you need to reclaim some mental space. Let your brain take a break! Breaks allow you to check in with yourself and refuel. Checking in helps you align with yourself as you step back, get some distance, remind yourself of your "why," and examine whether your thoughts, your words, and your actions are congruent.

European working culture generally allows for more downtime and vacation than North American—yet ubiquitous technology is making unplugging far more difficult everywhere, as email and cell phones follow us wherever we go. To make things worse, it is often difficult to switch off this cerebral hyperactivity, which no longer stays at the office. Instead, it shadows us in the evenings, on weekends, on holidays, and perhaps at night, disrupting our sleep. The benefits of a good vacation wear off after a few weeks.

How do you reclaim mental space in your daily life? Start by finding ways to refuel. We all recharge differently, besides the basic needs of proper food, sleep, and exercise. What gives you energy? One of my clients learned to take breathers between meetings, allowing herself to sit down for a few minutes and have a coffee on her way back to the office. Or perhaps listening to music for a few minutes works for you. Or stepping out of the office to walk and clear your head. Or talking to a friend.

An effective way to refuel and reclaim mental space is to suspend the past and the future and stand in the present moment. This ability to bring yourself back to the present is known as mindfulness. Mindfulness and other forms of meditation have been scientifically shown to be among the most effective techniques to reclaim that headspace. This is why many tech firms in Silicon Valley often start meetings with a few minutes of silence. It gives everyone in the room a chance to clear their heads and focus. But like anything else, the ability to stand in the present at will is a skill that requires practice. Google started nudging its staff to attend mindful meditation training as early as 2007,[1] and the practice has now spread far beyond Silicon Valley to traditional Fortune 500 companies such as Goldman Sachs and General Mills.[2]

Think of it as cerebral downtime, like a mini-holiday for the brain. Your energy settles into calm. This downtime pays off: a refreshed brain has been linked to higher attention, motivation, memory, and productivity[3]—all of which feed

How do you reclaim mental space in your daily life? Start by finding ways to refuel.

---

performance. Cerebral downtime also facilitates perspective and creativity: your unplugged brain is better able to make lateral connections that then bubble up to the surface of your consciousness, with inspiration seemingly coming out of the blue. Put simply, meditation helps rebalance attention away from your over-taxed frontal cortex and its analytical, linear, rational thinking towards your more intuitive self. Some studies have suggested that cerebral downtime is essential to staying connected with ourselves and with others, affirming our own identities and helping to understand human behavior.[4] In other words, it is essential to cultivate alignment with oneself and promote emotional intelligence.

Meditation has been shown to result in profound changes in brain structure over time, strengthening areas associated with emotional control, memory, introspection, attention, and abstract thought. When your brain takes a break, it does not stop working. Instead, it allows many mental processes to take place—just as essential physiological processes take place while you sleep. It makes space for the more intuitive part of your mind.

Some of you might be groaning right now. "Meditation? Really?" But before you visualize yourself wearing a robe and burning incense, please know that mindfulness does not require shaving your head and sitting in the lotus position for hours. It simply means to be present, fully aware of what you are doing—whether you are cooking, listening to music, walking, or staring at the ceiling. All you need to do is focus on something other than your thoughts. It can be your breath, or the sights or sounds around you. Find your own way of doing this. One of my clients cultivated mindfulness by going fishing, focusing on the sound of the wind rushing in the trees, the gentle ripple of the water, and his fishing line flying through the air. Another chose to listen to music, focusing on each instrument and the variations in the vocalist's voice. Once Bill, the hyperactive CEO, got over his fear of being alone with his thoughts, he worked on carving out short breaks during the day to reconnect with himself. For a few minutes, he would stop looking at his phone or email and do nothing. Before launching into a new idea, he asked himself whether it was aligned with his priorities. By slowing down his hectic mental activity, he gained much needed perspective—and effectiveness.

When Justine was trying to decide whether or not to get married, she connected with her intuition by taking time away from consciously thinking about that decision. She left her regular life for a couple of days and went to a hotel to be alone. Taking a break from obsessing over the pros and cons and allowing herself time to do nothing helped her clear her head. She gave her intuition space to come through. After a couple of days, she was ready to look at the situation with fresh eyes and quickly came to the decision to get married, which was in full alignment with herself.

Steve Jobs was famous for doing much of his creative thinking while taking walks. Inventor Thomas Edison's intuitive insights came to him when he was hovering between sleep and wakefulness. When confronted with a particularly sticky problem, he would sit in his chair with two steel balls in his hands, drifting towards sleep with a pad and pencil next to him. If he drifted too far, the noise of the balls falling out of his hands would wake him up. Albert Einstein and Salvador Dali also regularly wandered between sleep and full consciousness, a space where the linear and analytical part of their minds relaxed their grip, allowing intuition to flourish. Rock climbers credit the intense focus their sport requires for their ability to get some distance from their thoughts.

Place your hands on your lap, close your eyes, and focus on your environment for a few minutes. *Really focus.* Can you feel your feet planted on the ground? The back of your chair pressing against you? The palms of your hands on your legs? What sounds do you hear? What do you smell? Focus on your breathing. Every time you notice you have been distracted by thoughts, gently bring your mind back to the sounds and smells around you. Practice taking a few

———

Mindfulness does not require shaving your head and sitting in the lotus position for hours. It simply means to be present, fully aware of what you are doing.

———

moments to anchor yourself in the present, paying attention to what's around you, and you'll open the door to your intuition. If you haven't used it in a while, it may feel skittish and unpredictable, like a wild horse ready to bolt. It may take a little time before you're able to clear your mind and find a silent inner space. But if you keep practicing, it will help you stay aligned with yourself.

With that mental space nurtured, you'll be better able to stay focused and keep external influence in perspective—further cultivating your inner alignment. This is what we'll discuss in the coming chapter.

REFLECTIONS

Do you take breaks during the day to reconnect with yourself?

_____

Take a few minutes to focus on the now and on your surroundings. What do you see? What do you hear? What do you smell?

_____

_____

_____

_____

_____

Focus on your breathing for a few minutes. What happens when you do?

_____

_____

_____

_____

12

STAY FOCUSED
UNTIL YOU CROSS
THE FINISH LINE

WHILE NAVIGATING AN obstacle course, a rider on horseback always risks losing focus. A noise from the crowd or a sudden change of light may distract her, or perhaps her mind starts to wander. Her attention gets sidetracked from the overall path and strategy she'd set for the race. A jump going right or wrong can threaten her focus and concentration: when the jump is impeccable, she might take the rest of the race for granted and celebrate too early; if, on the other hand, her horse hits a bar, she might be mulling over what went wrong, how many points she's lost, or what she or her horse could have done differently. If the rider loses focus, her instructions and communication with her mount become less precise, and the horse does not respond as well. Ultimately, distraction takes the rider out of alignment with herself and with her horse well before the race is over. Most riders I know have made that mistake and sometimes missed crossing the finish line entirely, even after a perfect course. I once was so distracted that I missed the starting line.

What happens when leaders lose sight of their alignment? Imagine a vast volume of water. Unless channeled, that water spreads far and wide. Now visualize that same volume of water running through a dam. When properly channeled, water can produce electricity. Similarly, light can be diffuse and soft—or turn into laser. This is the power of focus.

The same is true in all areas of life. In business, leaders have to rely on their ability to ignore distractions and focus on what is most important. This is increasingly challenging as the role of business leader has grown in scope. Leaders have to balance demands on their time and attention from a multitude of constituencies: from their boards and collaborators to customers, suppliers, and other external partners. Meanwhile, markets and supply chains are becoming ever more global, and organizations more complex. Technology is disrupting traditional business models, creating opportunities but also uncertainties. The onslaught of information and data makes it more challenging to triage what's important: the hundreds of emails clogging your inbox? The latest headlines pinging on your phones? Stock prices? Twitter feeds? Who said what at a recent board meeting? A sudden crisis that needs immediate attention? The list goes on and on.

How you spend your time signals priorities to the rest of your team, which in turn determines their own focus— and what ultimately gets done.

Take email, for instance. According to a *Harvard Business Review* study, CEOs spend almost a quarter of their time on email, much of which doesn't need to involve them— it's endless FYI communication. Besides interrupting their work, it pulls CEOs into the operational weeds—all distractions. Furthermore, email sent by CEOs can easily cascade into a torrent of unnecessary communications, which then distracts everyone. When CEOs send email at night or on weekends, they send the signal that everyone should be working during their personal time. But many leaders still find email hard to avoid, even though they regard it as ineffective and a time sink.[1]

Unless leaders are able to prioritize their energy and attention, their impact gets severely diluted. Amid all the daily noise, it is easy to lose focus on where you want to go and why—and which levers to operate to get there.

How do you keep your focus and stay connected with your purpose in order to maintain your alignment?

First, be clear on where you can have an impact—and where you can't. Grant, a senior executive heading a department in a large financial services company, was distracted by all the daily noise. Buzzing like a fly in a jar, he spent an enormous amount of time and mindspace concerned with what his colleagues were saying or doing and wondering how to respond. Instead of concentrating on what was within his control, he also worried about what he could not change, such as stock prices and exchange rates. As he lost focus, so did his team. Priorities were fuzzy. Everyone's time and energy were dispersed, and any sense of collective alignment dissipated. The result? Grant was exhausted and stressed, and his impact and effectiveness suffered.

Our coaching work allowed him to regain some perspective. Once he was able to focus on what he could change—and let go of what he could not—he tapped into a sense of clarity and calm that had thus far eluded him. His communication became clearer as well, and his team fell into step with his newfound sense of focus.

Aligning how you spend your time with your clear priorities is a good way to stay focused and avoid getting distracted by the constant demands on your time and attention. Yet some leaders are better than others at doing so, and most find that time management is one of their greatest challenges. Time devoted to core agenda items varies from 14 per cent to 80 per cent of their working hours, according to the *Harvard Business Review* study. CEOs were dismayed to find out they spend only 3 per cent of their work time with customers, for example.[2] A clearly communicated agenda shared with direct collaborators helps leaders stay focused, since others become aligned to the common priorities. How you spend your time signals priorities to the rest of your team, which in turn determines their own focus—and what ultimately gets done.

Maintaining focus until the end means not taking your foot off the pedal too soon. In horseback riding, as in business, a race is not over until you've crossed the finish line.

Keeping a laser focus on the next obstacle as well as the finish line—while ignoring daily distractions and prioritizing competing demands on your time and attention—requires

Leaders have to rely on their ability to ignore distractions and focus on what is most important.

———————

commitment and practice. Carve out meaningful periods of alone time for reflection without interruption: although CEOs spend an average of 28 per cent of their work time alone, most of it is in short fragments of one hour or less.[3] Reconnect with your sense of purpose and why it is important to you. Doing so is like ascending above the skyline in a helicopter. Your view is no longer obstructed by the cars, the crowds, and the buildings. From this perspective, you are far better able to see the big picture. That clarity and perspective, combined with a healthy connection to your intuition, feeds confidence, keeps you focused, and makes decisions easier. Do the choices you make feel in line with what you want? Do they take you closer or farther away?

Think of a challenge you're facing. Ask yourself: what drives me? Are you still clear about your overall purpose, objective, and plan? Are you focusing on what you can impact? Or are you distracted and unsure about what priorities are? Is your calendar aligned with your priorities? Are you able to cordon off some alone time to clear the noise, refocus, and maintain your alignment?

Now that you've refined your inner alignment by moving past your self-limitations, cultivating positive emotions, dealing with setbacks productively, listening to your intuition, reclaiming some mental space, and keeping your focus, we'll discuss how this inner alignment connects with your environment.

REFLECTIONS

What is your sense of purpose?

_____

_____

_____

What do you do to stay connected to your purpose?

_____

_____

_____

What are your priorities? Please list them.

_____

_____

_____

On which of these priorities do you have the most impact?

_____

Check your calendar: how well are your priorities reflected? What can you do to adjust how you spend your time, if necessary?

_____

_____

_____

_____

How much time do you spend alone and without distraction every day?

☐ less than 1 minute
☐ 5 to 10 minutes
☐ 20 minutes
☐ more than 20 minutes

13

FIND ALIGNMENT WITH
YOUR ENVIRONMENT

Y OU HAVE NOW moved closer to inner alignment.
Unless you live in a bubble, you are not isolated from
the rest of the world and immune from its influence.
Does your environment—where you live, where you work,
and the people around you—facilitate that sense of alignment, or does it impede it?

When I first traveled to the United States as a teenager,
I felt like I had wings. Although I had grown up in France, I
was immediately far more energized in North America, as if
I had come home somehow. Though I'd grown up watching
movies about the Second World War and listening to my
grandmother's experience of German occupation, I felt a
connection to the United States, a country that I associated

with freedom, optimism, and the boundless possibilities of the American dream. These values—added to the inherent dynamism I discovered once I spent time there, first during the summer and a few years later while studying marketing at Northeastern University—felt like a natural fit that propelled me forward. I adopted the view, which became a lifelong value, that everything is possible.

This is exactly what Philippe Grall felt for Japan. Karate classes and an early interest in eastern philosophy fed an initial sense of alignment, in spite of the distance from his native Brittany. The connection was confirmed when he first traveled to Osaka many years later. Philippe eventually found a way to relocate to Japan and work for a Japanese company, and with that first piece in place, he gradually added other elements that created an environment that sustains his own alignment. People he's met have contributed to his supportive ecosystem by providing inspiration and positively influencing his choices. He nurtures office aesthetics that are in line with his work as an executive coach and provide a physical anchor to his sense of congruence. "To be aligned," he says, "I first create the environment in which I know I can stay aligned."

The sense of ease that you gain through alignment, both with yourself—seeing more clearly the kind of leader you truly are—and with your environment, gives you energy. The friction generated by misalignment, on the other hand, can suck the life force out of you. A tuned-up car consumes less fuel than one whose engine needs maintenance. Or think of the energy consumed by the friction of a conventional train against its rails, compared to a magnetic levitation train gliding through the air.

Do you feel like a maglev train or a tired diesel engine on rusty rails? Do the people around you, the corporate culture in which you work, and the place or country where you live share your values? This does not necessarily mean that people must be like you, think like you, or share a similar background. (I'll talk more about this in chapter 17.) Nor does it mean that you must find a perfect geography—there is no such thing. It means finding people, cultures, and places that support your "why," who you want to be, and how you choose to manifest both, because they resonate with and therefore amplify your sense of purpose. Then the full expression of the leader you are can best flourish.

So, first ask yourself: does my environment give me energy, or drain it away from me? Does it facilitate or hinder my inner alignment, feeling like wind at my back or in my face?

When I asked that question to Sarah, she didn't even have to think. The friction she experienced in her professional life took a lot out of her. It wasn't the company or the job itself: working in financial services aligned with her sense of purpose, and she was happy with her role, which leveraged her technical strengths. In Sarah's case, her sense of isolation was a drain. She had not managed to properly connect with colleagues and did not feel integrated within the company, which made her work more challenging.

If you're not in sync with where you live, where you work, or the people around you, what can you do to create

—————

Do the people around you, the corporate culture in which you work, and the place or country where you live share your values?

—————

glide rather than friction? Through coaching, Sarah realized that much of the misalignment she felt with her environment came from her own resistance. She could ease her sense of isolation by first changing her attitude and her communication, while staying true to herself. Over time, she was able to identify and cultivate common ground with several colleagues, which facilitated collaboration. Her new sense of inner alignment, coupled with her ability to find allies, gave her a sense of ease, which had previously eluded her. Not only did she gain energy, she also gained influence with her colleagues.

If your disconnect with your environment is more profound, radical changes may be warranted to find an environment better aligned with who you are. As Howard, in charge of human resources at a consumer goods company, worked on his inner alignment, he realized that his environment was fundamentally out of sync with who he was and what he wanted to do. He found little meaning in his largely administrative role and in the mission of the company he worked for. He also realized that he missed the energy that foreign horizons gave him. After returning from a few years living abroad, he had slipped back into a static persona while focusing on the domestic market. These were not things that could be fixed by staying where he was. Howard decided to leave his company and accepted a new role more meaningful to him, one with operational responsibilities in developing international markets. His new environment nourished him, and the contribution he now makes to his company and its people refueled his energy tank. In two years, Howard went from managing twenty-five people in three countries to a team of more than 200 people in fifteen countries, and he has been given a seat on the board.

But what happens when your environment changes, whether due to a decision you make or something beyond your control? Perhaps you take on a new role with a new team, or your company goes through a restructuring. Perhaps you change companies, or you are reassigned to a new country. What happens to your alignment then?

You have to adjust and find a new alignment. You have to change—while at the same time staying true to yourself. How does this work? It takes curiosity, openness, and flexibility.

It's a process that expatriates often face in an extreme form. Most of their environment changes: country, culture, colleagues, friends, and sometimes their company. But this change is something Darek Lenart, senior vice-president of human resources at Mastercard North America Markets embraces. For Darek, an international career is a way to stay nimble and build resilience—two essential assets for today's leaders.

It started with curiosity for Darek. Growing up behind the Iron Curtain, he was starved of foreign contacts. He longed to explore beyond his native Poland and discover what the rest of the world looked like. How did people live and think? How did businesses operate? He was given a chance to find out when he joined the human resources team of a pharmaceutical company headquartered in Croatia that operated throughout Eastern Europe. Darek first moved to Zagreb; later came a move to Geneva with

PepsiCo. Working in foreign countries with international teams, Darek had to stretch beyond his comfort zone and the cultural norms familiar to him. And then with the arrival of a baby, the stretch straddled work and home. All these changes were very tough for the first few months.

How did Darek find his balance in this unfamiliar environment? First, he realized that his initial feelings, uncomfortable as they were, were still fundamentally in alignment with his global outlook and curiosity. He wanted to have an international career and work in an international company, so this made him embrace the early discomfort, which he saw as part of his personal growth. In addition, he found advice, coaching, and support from his boss, who had also lived in several countries. Darek also connected with other Polish expatriates, sharing a common language and cultural background, which provided him with some grounding familiarity. Also essential were a desire to learn and a readiness to adjust his thinking and communication style. This meant first listening, asking questions, and observing without judgment to understand how his new surroundings operated. After a period of adjustment and observation, Darek would start to make decisions. Meanwhile, his desire to establish genuine, not superficial, connections with people of different nationalities, backgrounds, and professional tracks offered countless opportunities to grow and change—and ultimately align with his new environment.

Darek now lives and works in New York City, and he keeps building this sort of agility by constantly stretching

Can you find alignment by making small adjustments in your environment or in yourself, or are bigger changes in order?

---

beyond the familiar and adjusting to new environments—whether it is meeting new people or joining new organizations outside of work. As he puts it, "I can become a better professional by opening myself to new experiences."[1]

How do you remain true to yourself while going through all this stretching and adjusting? For Gregory Enjalbert, a railway industry international executive originally from France, it is about deciding what to adopt from each country, what to leave out, and what to contribute in return.[2] He remembers how, when he first started living outside of his home country, his views were somewhat inflexible. Being exposed to new customs, ideas, people, and environments eventually led him to question his convictions and become more open. Like Darek's, Gregory's initial stance is now to observe, listen, and understand. He has found that learning the local language, in addition to facilitating communication, opens a window to local mindsets, as particularities of speech often reflect local ways of thinking. Gregory even refrains from speaking his own language and chooses total immersion when he moves to a new country, in order to accelerate his adjustment.

Gregory is able to point out the qualities he values and embraced in each of the countries where he has lived. This has led to his evolution, while staying true to himself. After years of moving and adjusting to multiple countries, from Canada and Germany to China and Thailand, multiple new jobs and multiple new teams, he is now better able to discern universal values and aspirations to which he connects, underpinned by a wide diversity of customs.

Do you know what environment is best aligned with who you are? First, try to recognize it. Where, and with whom, do you feel your energy increase? What, or who, depletes you? Do you share the same purpose and values as your team, your peers, or your board? Or are you pulling in different and incompatible directions? Do you feel like the odd one out in your company and where you live? Can you find alignment by making small adjustments in your environment or in yourself, or are bigger changes in order? When you find yourself in a new environment, how do you align yourself with it?

In Part III, we'll discuss how you can leverage your personal alignment to foster a collective one, thereby boosting your effectiveness and impact as a leader.

REFLECTIONS

Think of your current environment—where you live, where you work, and the people around you. Does it give you energy or drain it from you?

_____

_____

_____

Where, and with whom, do you feel your energy increase? What, or who, depletes it?

_____

_____

_____

If your current environment feels like a drain, can you find alignment through small adjustments? Or do you feel fundamentally at odds?

_____

_____

_____

Think of times in your life when you changed environments. How did you adjust?

_____

_____

_____

PART THREE

Be the Leader You Can Be

"Aligned leadership comes not only from the congruence of who you are with what you feel, and what you think, but also with what you say and what you do in your relationship with others."

———————————

THROUGH PARTS I and II, you have worked on your inner alignment, gaining altitude and perspective. You now enjoy a clearer view of who you are, where you want to go, why, and how to get there. You've deployed your emotional intelligence. Now comes the next question: how do you put this version of yourself into practice as a leader? How do you approach the human dimension of leadership through the lens of alignment? Aligned leadership comes not only from the congruence of who you are with what you feel, and what you think, but also with what you say and what you do in your relationship with others.

This is what Part III is about: leveraging your inner alignment to facilitate the collective alignment of the individuals who make up your team or your organization—an *alignment of alignments*—thereby boosting your influence and impact as a leader. It is about translating your vision and thoughts into action and results, and steering your ship with influence. It is about exercising what David Hawkins defines as power, as opposed to force, by fostering the collective alignment of the constellation of people operating within your area of influence.

Collective alignment looks like a school of fish, effortlessly and instinctively swimming in the same direction. How do you inspire others to align behind a collective vision, purpose, and set of values? How do you bring people into your wake and sustain their engagement, so that together you are able to take a quantum leap? The following chapters examine how collective alignment relates to effective communication, your agility as a leader, the fostering and management of diversity, and your role as a leader-facilitator.

14

COMMUNICATE EFFECTIVELY

WHEN I WAS learning to ride horses, my father taught me an essential lesson: "If your horse is not responding properly, then you're not communicating effectively." Much of my training centered on fostering effective communication. I had to decide on a clear course of action, or my horse would sense my confusion. Did I know exactly where I wanted to go and how to get there? Did I have a plan to navigate the obstacles standing between the starting point and the finish line? Ahead of a race, I first surveyed the obstacle course and decided how to approach it; I strategized and visualized how my horse and I would run it. With a clear objective in mind, my effective communication was focused on technique and nurturing the relationship with my horse. Did my hands and legs send precise signals aligned with my plan? Was my body optimally positioned to help the horse respond to my instructions? Was I able to decipher the signals my horse sent me and adjust accordingly? The more precisely I communicated with my horse, the better she responded, and the more we trusted each other. The more we trusted each other, the better we communicated.

In leadership, as in horseback riding, collective alignment cannot happen without connection, and connection requires good communication. No one is able to read your mind, so you have to make sure you properly translate your thoughts into words. Good communication involves sharing a clear and inspiring sense of purpose and direction, formulating a strategy on how to get there, and clarifying everyone's role and contribution. It is through these three elements that you're likely to get the best out of your team and be an even more effective and inspiring leader.

Communication starts with purpose. Let's first go back to Simon Sinek's concept of the golden circle, discussed in chapter 3. The "why" at the center of his circle applies not only to your own individual sense of purpose but also to brands and companies. Sinek points to brands such as Apple to illustrate how that sense of purpose can inspire a quasi-cult following among consumers. The same can be said of coworkers: how each individual relates to their company's or team's collective purpose—and how their own personal "why" relates to it—influences how inspired and engaged they are. As Best Buy's Hubert Joly puts it, "Engaging individuals by appealing to what drives them personally can create irrationally great outcomes." Surveys

Effective communication means making it clear how everyone contributes to the collective sense of purpose.

———————

have highlighted how millennials in particular are looking for workplaces that focus on purpose, not just profit, and are aligned with their values.

This concept offers us a useful template for moving towards collective alignment with effective communication. Instead of focusing on the "what" and the "how," Sinek argues, communication must start with the "why"—the inner circle of deeper purpose—before moving through, and connecting with, the specifics of the outer rings. This requires not only a well-articulated collective purpose—something Sinek argues few companies have a good handle on—but also the ability to communicate it clearly, as well as the commitment to engage individuals on their personal "why" to bring them into collective alignment.

What does this mean for a business such as Best Buy? The company is not "about" selling TVs and computers after all—that is the "what." Best Buy redefined its purpose as enriching lives through technology. Not only did focusing on the "why" motivate Best Buy employees, it also expanded the company's potential market. The company could then address the needs of its customers in a broader range of areas, from entertainment and communication to food preparation and health, with hardware as well as services and solutions.

Best Buy's redefinition started with each member of the executive team sharing their personal "why" over dinner. A few months later, store managers and other field leaders were invited to share their own during an "all in—what drives you?" retreat. Joly credits the company's turnaround to the alignment between the company's purpose and what drives its employees. "The power it unleashes is phenomenal," he says. "Growing a business starts with 'why.' It starts with defining its bigger reason for being, and ensuring it is connected with what drives us as individuals."

I coached a CEO client who was brilliant, with a strong sense of purpose and a clear vision of where he wanted to take the company. He also had a plan for how to get there, which involved changing the company structure and incorporating new technologies. He was spending a lot of time and energy turning his plan into reality, acting like an all-capable Superman—flying from meeting to meeting, solving crises, pushing his reforms through while tending to clients. Busy as he was, he had little time to spend with his team, which languished. He could not understand why his team wasn't putting in more effort, and he felt he had to make it all happen himself. The trouble was that he had never taken the time to explain his intentions, his plan, and the bigger purpose and vision behind them. Having made no effort to bring everyone on board, he had very little leverage. He was left trying to do all the heavy lifting by himself, and his impact was limited.

Once he understood the value of communicating with his top team and encouraging them to do the same with their teams, he realized he didn't have to do it all. A shared sense of purpose fueled a spirit of belonging in the organization, which in turn fueled enthusiasm, initiative, and productivity. With everyone now pulling in the same direction, he no longer felt isolated and instead felt the power of having an entire organization behind him.

Besides sharing your vision and values to fire up those who can identify with them, effective communication also means making it clear how everyone contributes to the collective sense of purpose. Alexander, a top executive at an insurance company, initially struggled to grasp the value of connecting with his team and peers. To Alexander, communication meant passing on instructions. There was no empathy or rapport, just the strictly technical. Because he showed little interest in connecting with anyone at the office—let alone communicating how valuable everyone's contribution was—Alexander knew little about the people around him, and they knew little about him. They did not trust each other. Along with lacking a sense of purpose, his team felt unappreciated. The result? His team was uninspired, and productivity left much to be desired. Alexander was also isolated among his peers, and his ideas—no matter how good they might be—got little traction with his management as he found himself with no ally to support him. He didn't see how he had been contributing to the situation.

Once he worked on his own alignment, however, Alexander no longer asked why. Not only did the benefits of connecting with people become self-evident, but the connection became something he authentically desired, rather than actively avoided. From there he earned the respect of his team, who—finally armed with a clear sense of direction, cohesion, and the satisfaction of feeling valued—became far more dedicated, not only to him and to each other but to the common purpose they shared. Conflicts became easier to resolve. More people wanted to join his team. Better able to share his vision and ideas, Alexander carried far more weight on the board. No longer a task master, he became a leader who inspired others. The tangible result? His division's net profits increased by 10 per cent within one year.

Effective communication facilitates your own alignment with your environment, as well as a sense of belonging within your team, who become united by a shared sense of purpose. Without it, confusion takes over as rumors and gossip fill the vacuum, and everyone pulls in different directions. Good communication in service of collective alignment is particularly crucial when the going gets tough. Hubert Joly says that busy leaders trying to save troubled companies often overlook one crucial element: transparent

Good communication involves sharing a clear and inspiring sense of purpose and direction, formulating a strategy on how to get there, and clarifying everyone's role and contribution.

communication at all levels. Shortly after he took over the reins at the failing retailer, Joly started sending informative and inspiring staff notes to communicate broadly to the organization, as the company was going through difficult times. A question in such circumstances is how transparent and trusting to be, especially given the risk of leaks of confidential information. In this case, trust paid off. Virtually nothing leaked, and the Best Buy turnaround was fueled by well-informed employees.

"A well-informed workforce is vital for many reasons," says Joly. "But one of the most important reasons is the sad-but-true fact that turnarounds are not linear. There will be setbacks and failures and moments of concern, even doubt. The only hedge you have against those moments is a large group of employees educated enough about the 'what' and 'how' of the turnaround that they are willing to stick with it, even in the dark moments that will always occur."

As with any other skill, becoming an effective communicator requires practice, commitment, patience, and trust. How well do you communicate? Is everyone around you clear on the "why," the "what," and the "how" of their role? When was the last time someone understood something different than what you intended in your communication?

In the next chapter, we'll address another essential part of effective communication that fosters an alignment of alignments: listening, and how to adjust to the cues you pick up.

REFLECTIONS

What is your company's and/or your team's "why"? How does it align with your own?

_____

_____

_____

_____

How do you make sure that members of your team are aware of their collective purpose and how they each contribute to it?

_____

_____

_____

_____

How often do you communicate around the "why," the "what," and the "how" of their roles?

_____

_____

_____

_____

How, and how often, do you engage members of your team on their own individual purpose?

_____

_____

_____

_____

_____

_____

What can you do to communicate "from the inside out," following Simon Sinek's golden circle?

_____

_____

_____

_____

_____

15

LISTEN, ADJUST, AND FIND THE RHYTHM

HOW WELL DO you listen?

To be effective, communication has to go both ways. The equestrian and her mount must listen and "speak" to each other. To find and maintain perfect alignment, the rider must pick up cues from her horse and constantly adjust. If she has invested time and effort to get to know her horse, her course of action incorporates its attributes—strengths and weaknesses, likes and dislikes, the length of its step. The course of action also reflects the horse's mood on the day of the race. Is it confident and playful? Or nervous and tired? How are the terrain and weather conditions affecting her mount? The horse senses and responds to the equestrian's state of mind and attitude as well. Is she nervous or confident? Clear-minded or confused? Is she attentive? The horse will react accordingly, mirroring the rider's state of mind, creating an emotional loop. Riders don't have to look any further than their horses' behavior to find a reflection of their own emotions and the signals they unwittingly send.

This two-way communication continues throughout the race. Reality rarely matches even the best laid plans. A noise startles you or your mount; the length of the steps you had anticipated needs adjusting; something is not quite right. To excel, riders pick up on cues and know how and when to adjust. They listen to their horse and figure out whether the rhythm is appropriate. They are agile enough to correct their course and recalibrate their alignment.

In leadership situations, the effective communication essential to achieving and maintaining team alignment is not only about sharing a clear vision and purpose; it also involves active and instinctive listening, as well as making adjustments. Gone are the days when leaders were technical experts expected to have all the answers. Good leadership is now about asking the right questions and finding the best solutions by encouraging contributions, listening, and being able to hear what people may not be saying out loud. As one successful CEO once told me, "I have two ears and one mouth. This means, of course, that I spent much more time listening than speaking."

This takes practice and instinct, as communication can get distorted when you're in charge. Employees tend to tell their bosses what they want to hear and do things they believe will make their leaders happy. This often results in actions beyond what leaders intend, a situation organizational psychologist and bestselling author Robert Sutton calls "executive magnification." Sutton tells the story of an executive who innocently asked why there was a new door in a room. His team took it as a criticism and promptly plastered and painted over it. The executive had to clarify that he had not meant it as a criticism, and the door reappeared. Similarly, the CEO of a retail chain who had complained about a rude clerk found out two years later that, unbeknownst to him, his words had resulted in a costly campaign to improve employee courtesy—a campaign he'd never wanted in the first place.[1]

Leaders who encourage suggestions for improvement from their employees—and are genuinely open to hearing them—are rewarded with a boost in staff engagement and retention. This is not surprising: would you rather work on an initiative, project, or strategy that you have helped shape, or one in which you've had no input? How would you feel if your ideas and suggestions were never considered? A *Harvard Business Review* article describes the CEO of a desktop publishing software firm who routinely dismissed the advice of his senior colleagues, thinking he alone knew what was best for the company. Although brilliant, he was out of touch with market realities, and his inability to listen resulted in an exodus of his executive team. The company is now defunct.[2] This is not an isolated example: fewer than half of executives and managers frequently or always encourage suggestions for improvement.[3]

If all you get is sunny feedback, it's time to get skeptical and unearth what people might not be saying out loud.

Contrast this with the example of a technology research firm where the company's CEO always spoke last, listening to everyone's point of view before expressing his own. When asking his team to look into a problem, he refrained from advancing his own theory or suggestions, knowing that "the boss's answer" would stifle creativity and ownership, potentially nipping great new ideas in the bud.[4] This type of collaboration makes it easier not only to craft initial plans but also to navigate setbacks or obstacles, changing course if necessary. It nourishes a sense of collective belonging and engagement in a common purpose.

These are communication challenges that one of my clients, the CEO of a healthcare business, encountered firsthand when he decided to adjust his communication style. No one understood what he was doing or why, but he decided that he would share more, encourage collaboration and input, and listen. He called a meeting, communicated his strategy, and asked for collective feedback. "What do you think of the plan? Can we improve anything?" he asked. No one peeped, except to make vague acquiescing noises. "Everything is perfect!" he concluded. It took him a while to realize that it wasn't. If all you get is sunny feedback, it's time to get skeptical and unearth what people might not be saying out loud. There is no situation or plan that can't be improved. Is your team perhaps feeling it is too risky to speak up? Or do they believe that they will be ignored anyway?

The CEO then met with his top collaborators one by one, and he took more time to explain his vision and purpose, and why he felt that it was good for the company and its people. Then he rephrased his question: "Where do we have problems?" He challenged anyone who claimed there weren't any and convinced his team that he was genuinely interested in their input. He made space to listen. He started getting answers and contributions. To his surprise, he learned a lot; he'd been isolated from some realities. The feedback and discussions generated fresh ideas that improved his initial plan.

Asking for feedback and contributions means that you have to genuinely listen to the responses, be open to criticism, and be ready to act on valuable input. While genuine consultation improves the quality of decisions and buy-in, paying lip service to collaboration and then ultimately ignoring input is a sure way to discourage and demotivate your team.[5] Sham consultation is not listening, and no one likes to be taken for a ride.

How can you encourage people reporting to you to speak up? Are you willing to acknowledge your fallibility, as Aicha Evans did when Intel's SoFIA initiative flopped? Or are you worried this might weaken your position? Communicating that you don't have all the answers—and therefore you need your collaborators on board—contributes to what Amy Edmondson, professor of leadership and management at Harvard Business School, calls "psychological safety": a work environment in which people trust that they can speak up because they know they won't be punished or ridiculed for doing so. As a leader, be curious and ask a lot of questions. Communicate that everyone's contribution is valuable, especially in an increasingly complex and uncertain business environment. Edmondson argues that, coupled with accountability, this type of environment creates high-performing teams.[6]

Google agrees. For two years, the tech giant looked into what makes their teams effective, relying on rigorous data and analysis. What was the number one factor? Feeling safe to take risks and be vulnerable in front of each other—psychological safety. The qualifications on the team turn out to be far less important than how people on that team interact.[7] When people are not afraid to speak up or ask questions, mistakes and flawed practices get rooted out, while learning and innovation flourish.

Nurturing trust and psychological safety also help to create an environment in which people are not afraid to fail,

———

As a leader, be
curious and ask
a lot of questions.
Communicate
that everyone's
contribution is
valuable.

———

because no one gets ridiculed, shamed, rejected, or punished for making mistakes. Only then can setbacks be used as learning moments and be built upon. As noted in chapter 9, it starts with projecting a growth mindset and your own attitude towards setbacks. For Aicha Evans, creating psychological safety requires checking in with her team, particularly when things get hard. "It's top of mind almost every day." No one should assume that because one person feels safe, others do too. Evans also acknowledges with her team that although they may know where to start when working towards an objective, they don't have to have it all figured out. When confronted with setbacks, they will test, adapt, and learn together to figure out how to move forward. She also establishes what she calls "boundary conditions": mapping out with her team the best- and worst-case scenarios and how to handle it if either were to materialize.

The right questions and active listening shine a light not only on each individual's sense of purpose but also on their talents and areas of growth; this approach also reveals what kind of leadership and communication style might be most effective for them. Surveys from The Culture Works, a company specialized in employee engagement, show that motivators change with age. For instance, autonomy becomes increasingly more important the older team members are, whereas recognition is far more important to their younger colleagues. Some might excel with clear objectives and wide elbow room while getting there. Others may crave more guidance. What motivates each team member? How can you best facilitate their growth and learning? When you're at peace with who you are and value your own specific talents, it becomes much easier to recognize and value those of others and, like a coach, support and facilitate their development. "The primary responsibility of managers is to care about the success and well-being of their people," says Adam Grant, bestselling author and organizational psychologist at the Wharton School. "If you don't have time to talk individually each week with each of your direct reports, you have too many direct reports."[8] Getting to know your team this way allows you to foster a sense of belonging, to spot outliers, and to better understand the human resources you can work with—all of which facilitates team alignment.

Are you asking the right questions, listening enough, and getting input from your team? How well do you take feedback? How do you communicate about failure? Do you notice when something might be left unsaid? Can you identify your collaborators' needs and how they prefer to be managed? Are you able to adjust your communication and leadership style accordingly?

Now that we've discussed the role of communication and agility in aligning your team, we'll cover how to further that collective alignment while promoting diversity.

REFLECTIONS

How often do you ask questions? How do you incorporate others' input in your plans?

_____

_____

_____

_____

How do you encourage feedback and contributions from your team and colleagues? How do you react to them?

_____

_____

_____

_____

How do you adjust your communication and leadership style depending on who is in front of you?

_____

_____

_____

_____

How do you encourage the growth and development of team members?

_____

_____

_____

_____

What do you do to foster psychological safety in your team? How do you react to setback and failure within your team? How do you acknowledge your own weaknesses and fallibility?

_____

_____

_____

_____

_____

16

EMBRACE DIVERSITY

HOW CAN YOU nurture collective alignment while encouraging diversity?

When dealing with cultures, modes of thinking, backgrounds, or outlooks different from our own, creating and maintaining alignment by communicating effectively and adjusting to new circumstances or environments is particularly crucial—and challenging. It's important to note that alignment does not mean pressuring others to think and behave the same way we do, or becoming someone we are not in order to fit in. Instead it involves cultivating the agility and openness to embrace, foster, and leverage diversity.

This agility has become an imperative for leaders. Marshall Goldsmith argues that managing diversity has become one of the most important qualities leaders must have to succeed. Why? Because leaders increasingly have to think globally and facilitate partnerships.[1] Embracing diversity of all kinds—from gender, race, and sexual orientation to age, experience, culture, or cognitive penchant—has been shown to impact the bottom line. Those with a more diverse leadership perform better than average financially.[2]

I learned the value of diversity after I started my own business in the steel industry. My business partner and I could not have been more different: he was a self-made industrial entrepreneur who knew the industry by heart and had a talent for everything technical; my career had focused on advertising for luxury brands, along with marketing and media with large companies. Yet he convinced me that the fresh perspective and the marketing approach I brought to the table would be very valuable. After talking to a trader, my business partner and I identified a market need: we built a business helping small foundries recycle and reuse scraps from expensive raw material, helping both their bottom line and the environment. I ended up leading a company of engineers doing research to develop new technologies in an industry I initially knew nothing about. I was also a woman in a sector overwhelmingly dominated by men. But at our company, everyone knew that we all brought something different to the table, and we valued everyone's contribution. I learned a lot about chemistry from our engineers, and they learned about marketing from me. Working together, we came up with far more innovative approaches and solutions.

Why are companies that embrace diversity doing better? First, as I experienced firsthand in my own business, diverse teams tend to result in better decisions and more innovation. Learning, reasoning, and problem-solving happen in different ways for different people. Frameworks such as Myers-Briggs and DISC, for example, identify various cognitive styles, which in turn facilitate understanding across differences. In *Quiet: The Power of Introverts in a World that Can't Stop Talking*, Susan Cain makes the case that western business culture, which has favored and rewarded extroversion, would benefit from embracing the many qualities that introverts bring to the table.

How does diversity relate to innovation? IBM's Jennifer Paylor argues that innovation comes from disrupting one's own thinking. And what better way to do that than to collaborate with people who do not think like you? Though it may be easier and more comfortable to interact with people who think like us and have a similar background, it doesn't stretch us outside of our box. We keep treading the same mental paths without being challenged. By contrast, being exposed to multiple cultures has been shown to boost creativity, as it allows us to consider and combine different perspectives.[3]

Aicha Evans (who has moved from Intel to Zoox, a driverless car startup) points out that this starts with you: "You have to first agree that there are people out there who are smarter than you or who have a better idea." These people are likely to be different from you in the way they think and in their experience. Gender, age, cultural, or racial diversity reflects different experiences.

More diverse companies are also better able to serve increasingly heterogeneous markets. Workforces that do

Being exposed to
multiple cultures
has been shown
to boost creativity,
as it allows us
to consider and
combine different
perspectives.

not reflect the diversity of their customers are unlikely to come up with products and services aligned with the people they are meant to serve. They succumb to the unconscious biases we all have, and results range from irritating to downright dangerous. Facial recognition software, for instance, has been shown to work far better on white male faces than either female or darker skinned ones.[4] Why? Largely because the software reflects the demographic characteristics of developers and the data sets they use for machine learning: one popular facial recognition dataset, for example, was found to include more than three-quarters men and more than 80 per cent Caucasians. This is something Google learned the hard way when its Google Photos app, which helps users categorize and search their photos for people, places, or things, labeled darker-skinned faces as gorillas. As facial recognition software is being used for an increasing number of applications, ranging from marketing and recruitment to law enforcement, the consequences of this inherent bias could be catastrophic.

Artificial intelligence relies on training: exposing the system to a multitude of data sets, which often contain biases. The more diverse the team, the lower the risk of such biases being baked in and left undetected. "It really starts with people," says computer scientist Joy Buolamwini. "So, who codes matters. Are we creating full-spectrum teams with diverse individuals who can check each other's blind spots?"[5]

The challenges faced by female entrepreneurs is another example. The difficulties they face in raising capital has been partly attributed to the overwhelming domination of male venture capitalists and investors. The problem? Surrounded by too many people like themselves, investors are not always able to recognize their own biases or grasp business opportunities that target a demographic outside of their own. In her memoir *Shark Tales*, real estate entrepreneur turned investor Barbara Corcoran illustrates that very challenge. As the only female investor on *Shark Tank*, the American television show in which entrepreneurs pitch their ideas, she was the only one to understand the potential of a medication dispenser for toddlers shaped like an elephant. She concludes in her book that her male colleagues were most likely oblivious to the challenge of giving a sick infant medicine in the middle of the night. She was the only one supporting the venture, which became very successful. In a country such as the UK, women make 80 per cent of consumer purchases, yet they account for only 12 per cent of executive teams in companies surveyed by global consultancy McKinsey & Company.[6]

Fostering diversity also helps to recruit and retain talent. Leaders committed to hiring a diverse workforce can fish in a much bigger talent pond. Furthermore, a broader range of recruits feels at home in more diverse companies, which in turn improves their satisfaction and desire to stay. A 2017 Gallup survey revealed that fostering environments that celebrate diversity greatly improves employee engagement.[7] Diversity is particularly valued among younger generations: almost half of millennials consider diversity and inclusion important criteria when considering a potential employer.[8]

How can diversity be nurtured? First, measure it. As Peter Drucker would say, you can't improve what you don't measure. An increasing number of companies include diversity as factors in assessing leadership performance and weave diversity training and coaching into the corporate culture. Inspired by the example of top orchestras, which have introduced blind auditions for musicians, more measurable and objective criteria have been introduced in recruiting and promoting to keep biases in check.

Hubert Joly argues that creating an environment in which every employee can be themselves, grow, and feel valued is an intrinsic part of leadership and management. Best Buy's strategy has been to foster diversity and inclusivity along four axes: workforce, workplace, suppliers, and community. Diversifying recruitment pipelines, for instance, ensures that the company hires more diverse talent, and social benefits have been reviewed to take into consideration diverse situations and needs, from childcare to gender transitioning.

Creating diversity, however, is not enough in itself. If it is to produce the benefits outlined above, diversity needs to be actively managed so that it feeds, rather than hinders, collective alignment. Jim Turley, the former CEO of Ernst & Young, draws an important distinction: "Diversity itself is about the mix of people you have, and creating an inclusive culture is about making that mix work."[9] Aicha Evans agrees that seeking out people different from us is only the first step: because we have a natural tendency to align with the similar, inclusion does not happen by itself but requires systems and efforts.

Because we have a natural tendency to align with the similar, inclusion does not happen by itself but requires systems and efforts.

What does "making the mix work" involve? It requires alignment on several levels. First, align teams around common values and purpose—including diversity itself. Looking back at the business I co-created, the glue that brought us together, in spite of our many differences, was our collective desire to find the best possible solutions for our clients. We shared a common purpose of helping small foundries compete in a sector dominated by large corporations, while respecting the environment. In addition, we all recognized and valued each and everyone's unique contribution.

"Cultural brokers"—staff who are able to facilitate interactions and communication among people of diverse backgrounds—can help provide the glue that makes the mix work by integrating or eliciting knowledge from different cultures.[10] Sometimes, it also boils down to the right structure and incentives. Best Buy, for example, has put in place a number of initiatives meant to actively manage diversity and facilitate inclusion. For instance, each member of the leadership team meets monthly with a "reverse mentor"—someone from a different ethnic, age, or social background—to help broaden perspectives. Joly also points out how facilitating new kinds of interactions—for example, having small groups cook a meal together—helps people see their colleagues in a different light and facilitates connections.

Ultimately, CEOs who run organizations recognized for embracing people of different backgrounds see diversity not only as a business imperative but also as a moral one. They approach it as a personal mission central to their own values, often rooted in their experience of what it means to be an outsider.[11] In other words, they are personally aligned with diversity and inclusion and why they matter, which in turn helps root these values within their organizations and align their teams too.

How important is diversity to you? Are you clear on how much you value it? What can you do to foster it around you and in your organization? Are you aware of your own biases? What are you doing to facilitate inclusion? How do you promote collective alignment through diversity?

In the final chapter, we'll conclude by discussing how the inner and collective alignment you've nurtured allows you to be a leader-facilitator.

REFLECTIONS

What do you do to encourage diversity (gender, age, experience, cognitive approach, etc.) in your team?

_____

_____

_____

_____

How do you correct for your own biases?

_____

_____

_____

_____

How do you facilitate inclusion and collective alignment?

_____

_____

_____

_____

17

THE ART OF LETTING GO

AS A LEADER, how tightly do you hold on to the reins? A good equestrian knows that once she has aligned with her horse and prepared for the jump, she must let go. She has surveyed the obstacle course, communicated and listened effectively, established trust, and found the right cadence to position herself at the optimum position to jump. Now what? Here, the rider's only job is to let the horse take off. The equestrian trusts herself and her horse, and she is confident that both are ready to play their parts. She knows her role is to focus on adjusting her balance and body position in order to facilitate, rather than hinder, her mount's performance. Her role is also to look ahead and anticipate the next obstacle.

The same goes for leaders. Marshall Goldsmith argues that to be effective in today's and tomorrow's business environments, leaders must increasingly take on the role of facilitators, rather than experts telling people what to do and how to do it.[1] Assembling, inspiring, and positioning a cohesive and diverse team to successfully navigate obstacles produces far better results than when a leader pushes individuals over the humps, especially in a context of rapid technological change, heightened uncertainty, and accelerating globalization. The former approach also requires far less energy. As covered in the preceding chapters, your role as a leader is to inspire by communicating a sense of collective purpose and values that align with your team's "why," to encourage cohesion and diversity within your team (as well as its alignment with the outside world), and to promote mutual trust. Positioning your team in such an optimal way allows your collaborators to do their jobs, while you keep looking forward. Creating this collective alignment allows you to be, in the words of Marshall Goldsmith, a facilitator.

Without all these pieces in alignment, however, letting go is ineffective. If you fail to define and communicate an inspiring collective purpose, and to recruit collaborators who are motivated by it, your team will likely be disengaged. Instead of facilitating, you'll find yourself doing the heavy lifting. This was the case for my client Ivan, the energetic CEO of a financial services company. Nursing an innovative vision for how to modernize and reposition the business he was leading, he ended up doing much of the execution as well, dealing with clients, handling crises, and staying

Leaders become successful by facilitating the success of others.

---

involved in every aspect of the business. Instead of supporting his collaborators in doing their work, he was doing it for them.

If you don't trust your team, or your team doesn't trust you, you can't let go. After he became COO of a distribution company, Gus overshadowed everyone. He relied on his substantial intellect, rather than on his collaborators', to come up with solutions to every problem, feeling he was the most able to do so. Until he started being coached, he didn't rely on his team of senior executives, let alone their teams, as he ultimately felt that they were not as qualified as he was.

Are you confident that your team will deliver? Do you have the right people? Do you trust their ability, expertise, and judgment? Do you hold them accountable? Are they

———

Your role as a leader is to inspire by communicating a sense of collective purpose and values that align with your team's "why."

———

fired up and driven by a sense of purpose? If the answer to these questions is no, then some hard choices may have to be made to find collaborators you can lean on. In a study conducted by the *Harvard Business Review*, CEOs who had been in office for a while revealed that their number one regret was not setting high enough standards in selecting direct reports. When they had taken on the role of CEO, they focused too much on the present and not enough on the future: they therefore relied on people who were qualified for managing the status quo but not always capable of helping the company leap to the next level.[2]

Finding inner alignment and clarity about your own strengths makes it easier to recognize and appreciate the talents of others, facilitate their success by arranging the support they need, and ultimately loosen excessive control and empower them do their job. This does not always come naturally: many successful leaders find it hard to let go of the drive to prove that they are the best at everything. Changing roles requires adjustments. When you have stepped into more senior leadership roles, have you managed to step back from the execution and technical expertise that had thus far earned you kudos and success in order to embrace facilitation? Many of my clients rely on coaching to help them make that transition faster and better. Entrepreneurs who have bootstrapped a start-up and been involved in every detail do not always make good CEOs once the business takes off. This is a shift one of my clients, a successful entrepreneur who kept micromanaging business development even after he hired people to handle it, had to learn. Unable to handle the load after he parted ways with his business partner, he had to restructure and step into the role of leader-facilitator.

Yvon Chouinard, the founder of outdoor clothing brand Patagonia, is a master at letting go. In fact, he spends five months of the year out of the office. From June to November, he's off in Jackson Hole, fishing every day and pursuing his passion for the outdoors. He calls in only three or four times during his absence. "People know that if the warehouse burns down, don't call me. What can I do? You know what to do," he says. "Ant colonies don't have bosses. Everybody knows what their job is and they get the job done." Chouinard's view is that top-down management takes a tremendous amount of effort, and he instituted what he thinks is a better structure: "What we decided to do is just hire motivated, young, independent people and leave them alone." The company's policy is, when the surf comes up, people can drop work and go surfing—as long as the job gets done. Would that work everywhere? No, Chouinard argues, because it relies on finding the right people from the very beginning. In fact, a psychologist who studied Patagonia employees concluded that they are so independent that they would be unemployable anywhere else.[3]

Chouinard can hold the steering wheel with a very light touch at Patagonia because his fiercely independent hires are closely aligned with his vision and values. A surfer, mountain climber, and environmental activist himself, Chouinard has built Patagonia from the get-go to reflect his conviction that there is a different, more sustainable way of doing business. He created Patagonia to make rock climbing gear and outdoor clothing that he and his climbing and surfing pals wanted to use but couldn't find. Despite Patagonia's success, Chouinard is not chasing growth or short-term gains but rather longevity—for both the company and its products. Patagonia hardly advertises and does not encourage customers to buy more and more often, but rather fewer things that will last longer. By building a company and a team closely aligned with his own values, Chouinard has become the epitome of the leader-facilitator.

Effective leader-facilitators are similar to coaches. As an executive coach, I don't find answers for my clients. Rather, my job is to ask the right questions and provide the tools that will help them find their own answers and become more successful. Their success feeds my own success. Similarly, leaders become successful by facilitating the success of others.

Nurturing inner and collective alignment allows you to let go and facilitate, rather than instruct and do. And by letting go, you are able to focus on your role, which is to maintain a clear sense of collective purpose, set the strategic direction, and keep looking ahead.

Have you managed to create a collective alignment of individual alignments? Have you aligned yourself and your team so you're able to let go?

REFLECTIONS

How much do you trust your team and its ability to deliver? How much do you trust your collaborators' expertise, judgment, and commitment?

_____

_____

_____

How do you empower your collaborators to do their job? What do you do to facilitate their success? How invested are you in their growth?

_____

_____

_____

_____

What actions can you take to become even more of a leader-facilitator?

_____

_____

_____

CONCLUSION

ONE TYPE OF horse-riding competition pairs jumpers with horses they do not know. With no prior relationship, riders have to fall back on their extensive training, their ability to listen, and a heightened intuition to pick up cues and "read" the horses as they race. The best riders establish trust and connection within seconds, quickly finding the sweet spot where both rider and horse—each with their own particularities—can connect. In every new race, they are able to gauge the situation at lightning speed and find alignment without bending the horse to their will. These nimble and agile equestrians are able to find alignment in uncertainty and constant change.

The same goes with inner and collective alignment in life. Seeking and maintaining alignment is a practice and a process, not a one-off destination. Why? Because nothing ever stays the same—neither your environment nor yourself. Change happens ever faster, as technological leaps create a future we cannot yet imagine. Products and services in all sectors, as well as the way we do business, are undergoing massive disruptions. New generations with different mindsets and priorities enter the workforce and join the ranks of consumers, making their mark on the world and shaping how talent gets managed and markets served. What is true today won't be true tomorrow. You also keep growing and evolving, always stretching towards new destinations and challenges. Every situation, every setback, and every triumph call for a new you. And in the words of Marshall Goldsmith, what got you here won't get you there. You are faced with the choice of striving towards the leader you want to be—always pushing the goal posts a bit further— or stagnating.

More than ever, leaders must be nimble, anticipate changes, adjust, and embrace their responsibilities not only towards people within their organizations but also suppliers, customers, and the communities in which they operate. This requires continuously aligning and realigning with themselves and with the world around them. Marshall Goldsmith points out that in order to be successful in tomorrow's world, leaders have to embrace global thinking and cross-cultural diversity, understand rapidly changing technology and its impact, rely far more on alliances and partnerships than in the past, and be facilitators rather than experts. All of this requires agility, speed, and foresight. In this context, the ability to find and maintain alignment within oneself and with others becomes even more crucial—and also challenging. It is easy to drift away; a gifted entrepreneur I know once compared it to the imperceptible changes that we all miss looking at ourselves in the mirror every morning. It is only when we look at old photographs that we notice how these daily changes have accumulated to make a noticeable difference.

The path outlined in these pages has been applied to the context of leadership but defined in a broad sense, whether you are heading a multinational or charting the course of your own destiny. Alignment is indeed a concept that permeates all aspects of your life: professional and personal, as well as physical, emotional, and spiritual. Seeking it in one area of your life will invariably echo in all others. For you are not siloed but one; alignment is not contained but whole. Who you are at work cannot be divorced from who you are at home, and vice versa. Searching for and maintaining alignment as a leader reverberates in other roles you might fulfill in your life as well—be it a parent, friend, neighbor, or spouse. As Peter Drucker put it, satisfied, contented people are people that have lived in more than one world: "Those single-minded people—you meet them most in politics—in the end are very unhappy people."[1]

Alignment is a practice. With time, we refine the skill of sensing when we drift away from it, and we become better at finding it again. To hone that skill, I suggest you rely on a daily practice of carefully selected and crafted questions. This powerful and miraculous tool keeps you focused on what you want to change or improve. Start with one or two questions. What is it you'd like to work on first and foremost? It could be something as straightforward as exercising or healthy eating, or something more complex, like communicating from the inside out of Simon Sinek's golden circle. You'll find a list of suggestions for daily questions on my website, www.hortenselegentil.com. Pick the most relevant question, or make up your own. Every day, ask yourself, "Have I done my best today to move closer to what I set out to do or be?" Keep going for several months.

Over time, as your new habits take root, add new questions to the existing ones. I now have more than twenty daily questions. Most are reminders to make sure old hang-ups don't creep back in.

Alignment remains a work in progress as we keep growing, learning, and stretching our own limits. But it does not feel like work, because this is a most fulfilling quest. Once you've tasted the gift of alignment and the endless possibilities that come with it, you won't want to lead—or live your life—without it.

What better gift can you give yourself and the world than being your best you?

NOTES

CHAPTER 1: MIND THE GAP

1. The names and identifying details of coaching clients have been modified to respect their privacy.

CHAPTER 2: MIRROR, MIRROR ON THE WALL

1. "Meet the coaches behind the world's best Olympic teams," BBC. com. August 14, 2012. bbc.com/sport/olympics/19253531.
2. Rachel Nuwer, "Coaching Can Make or Break an Olympic Athlete," *Scientific American* online. August 5, 2016. scientificamerican.com/ article/coaching-can-make-or-break-an-olympic-athlete/.
3. Atul Gawande, "Want to Get Great at Something? Get a Coach," TED2017. Online video. ted.com/talks/ atul_gawande_want_to_get_great_at_something_get_a_coach.
4. Tim Theeboom, Bianca Beersma, and Annelies E.M. van Vianen, "Does coaching work? A meta-analysis on the effects of coaching on individ-ual level outcomes in an organizational context," *The Journal of Positive Psychology* 9:1 (2014), 1–18. doi.org/10.1080/17439760.2013.837499.
5. All quotations and references to Jennifer Paylor are drawn from the author's interview with her.
6. Adam Lashinsky, "Best Advice I Ever Got: Eric Schmidt: Hire a Coach," *Fortune* online. July 8, 2009. archive.fortune.com/galleries/2009/ fortune/0906/gallery.best_advice_i_ever_got2.fortune/14.html.
7. All quotations and references to Hubert Joly are drawn from the author's interview with him.

CHAPTER 3: CONNECT WITH YOUR "WHY"

1. Simon Sinek, "How Great Leaders Inspire Action," TEDx-Puget Sound, September 2009. Online video. ted.com/talks/simon_sinek_how_great_leaders_inspire_action.
2. Bill George is the former CEO of Medtronic and a fellow of Harvard Business School where he teaches leadership in executive education programs. He is the author of four bestselling books: *True North*, *Authentic Leadership*, *Finding Your True North*, and *7 Lessons for Leading in Crisis*.

CHAPTER 4: WHO DO YOU ASPIRE TO BE?

1. Hortense le Gentil, "How I Discovered the Leader I Am," *Leader to Leader* 89 (April 12, 2018): 51–55. doi.org/10.1002/ltl.20367.

CHAPTER 6: IDENTIFY YOUR SELF-LIMITATIONS

1. Tasha Eurich, *Insight: The Surprising Truth About How Others See Us, How We See Ourselves, and Why the Answers Matter More Than We Think*. New York: Crown Business, 2017.

CHAPTER 8: THE POWER OF POSITIVE EMOTIONS

1. Shawn Achor, *The Happiness Advantage: How a Positive Brain Fuels Success in Work and Life*. New York: Currency, 2010.
2. David R. Hawkins, *Power vs. Force: The Hidden Determinants of Human Behavior*. West Sedona, AZ: Veritas Publishing, 2012.

CHAPTER 9: THE GIFT OF "FAILURE"

1. Museum of Failure website, museumoffailure.se.
2. All quotations and references to Aicha Evans are drawn from the author's interview with her.
3. Carol S. Dweck , *Mindset: The New Psychology of Success*. New York: Random House, 2006.

CHAPTER 10: VALUE YOUR INTUITION

1. Antoine Bechara, Hanna Damasio, Daniel Tranel and Antonio R. Damasio, "Deciding advantageously before knowing the advantageous strategy," *Science* 275 (February 28, 1997): 1293–1295. labsi. org/cognitive/Becharaetal1997.pdf.
2. Ap Dijksterhuis, Maarten W. Bos, Loran F. Nordgren, Rick B. van Baaren, "On making the right choice: the deliberation-without-attention effect," *Science* 311 (February 17, 2006): 1005–1007. doi. org/10.1126/science.1121629.
3. Steven Kotler and Jamie Wheal, *Stealing Fire: How Silicon Valley, the Navy SEALs, and Maverick Scientists Are Revolutionizing the Way We Live and Work.* New York: Dey Street Books, 2017.
4. Daniel Goleman website. March 16, 2016. danielgoleman.info/ books/emotional-intelligence/.
5. Jacques Fradin, "Decider en comite de direction." Institut de NeuroCognitivisme. Online video, July 10, 2015. youtu.be/koLIKtahkt4.
6. Richard Delaye, "Napoléon ou quand la chance et l'intuition deviennent des outils d'aide a la décision," *La Tribune*, March 2, 2017. latribune.fr/opinions/tribunes/napoleon-ou-quand-la-chance-et-l-intuition-deviennent-des-outils-d-aide-a-la-decision-651460.html.

CHAPTER 11: RECLAIM SOME MINDSPACE

1. Brad Stulberg and Steve Magness, "How Googlers avoid burnout (and secretly boost creativity)," *Wired*, June 11, 2017. wired.com/ story/googlers-avoid-burnout-secretly-boost-creativity/.
2. Marissa Levin, "Why Google, Nike and Apple love mindfulness training, and how you can easily love it too," *Inc.*, June 12, 2017. inc. com/marissa-levin/why-google-nike-and-apple-love-mindfulness-training-and-how-you-can-easily-love-.html.
3. Ferris Jabr, "Why your brain needs more downtime," *Scientific American*, October 15, 2013. scientificamerican.com/article/ mental-downtime/.
4. Mary Helen Immordino-Yang, Joanna A. Christodoulou, and Vanessa Singh, "Rest is not idleness," *Perspectives on Psychological Science* 7(4): 352–364. doi.org/10.1177/1745691612447308.

CHAPTER 12: STAY FOCUSED UNTIL YOU CROSS THE FINISH LINE

1. Michael E. Porter and Nitin Nohria, "How CEOs Manage Time," *Harvard Business Review*, July–August 2018. hbr.org/2018/07/the-leaders-calendar.
2. Ibid.
3. Ibid.

CHAPTER 13: FIND ALIGNMENT WITH YOUR ENVIRONMENT

1. All quotations and references to Darek Lenart are drawn from the author's interview with him.
2. All quotations and references to Gregory Enjalbert are drawn from the author's interview with him.

CHAPTER 15: LISTEN, ADJUST, AND FIND THE RHYTHM

1. Robert Sutton, "How Bosses Waste Their Employees' Time," *Wall Street Journal*, August 12, 2018. wsj.com/articles/how-bosses-waste-their-employees-time-1534126140.
2. John Hamm, "The Five Messages Leaders Must Manage," *Harvard Business Review*, May 2006. hbr.org/2006/05/the-five-messages-leaders-must-manage.
3. Mark Murphy, "Only 1 Out of 4 Leaders Encourage Suggestions from Their Employees, New Data Shows," *Forbes*, October 22, 2017. forbes.com/sites/markmurphy/2017/10/22/only-1-out-of-4-leaders-encourages-suggestions-from-their-employees-new-data-shows.
4. Ibid.
5. Robert Sutton, "The Biggest Mistakes Bosses Make When Making Decisions—and How to Avoid Them," *Wall Street Journal*, October 29, 2018. wsj.com/articles/the-biggest-mistakes-bosses-make-when-making-decisionsand-how-to-avoid-them-1540865340.
6. Amy Edmondson, "Building a psychologically safe workplace, TEDxHGSE," TEDx Talks, May 4, 2014. Online video. youtu.be/LhoLuui9gX8.
7. Julia Rozovsky, "The five keys to a successful Google team," re:Work, November 17, 2015. rework.withgoogle.com/blog/five-keys-to-a-successful-google-team/.
8. Adam Grant, LinkenIn.com post. linkedin.com/feed/update/urn:li:activity:6463380581307727872/.

1. Interview with the author.
2. Vivian Hunt, Dennis Layton and Sara Prince, "Diversity Matters," McKinsey & Company, February 2, 2015. mckinsey.com/~/media/ mckinsey/business%20functions/organization/our%20insights/ why%20diversity%20matters/diversity%20matters.ashx.
3. Carmit Tadmor, Adam Galinsky, and William Maddux, "Getting the Most out of Living Abroad: Biculturalism and Integrative Complexity as Key Drivers of Creative and Professional Success," *Journal of Personality and Social Psychology* 103 3 (September 2012): 520–542. doi.org/ 0.1037/a0029360.
4. Steve Lohr, "Facial Recognition Is Accurate, if You're a White Guy," *New York Times*, February 9, 2018. nytimes.com/2018/02/09/technology/facial-recognition-race-artificial-intelligence.html.
5. Joy Buolamwini, "How I'm fighting bias in algorithms," TEDxBeaconStreet, November 2016. Online video. ted.com/talks/ joy_buolamwini_how_i_m_fighting_bias_in_algorithms.
6. Vivian Hunt, Dennis Layton and Sara Prince, "Diversity Matters," McKinsey & Company, February 2, 2015. mckinsey.com/~/media/ mckinsey/business%20functions/organization/our%20insights/ why%20diversity%20matters/diversity%20matters.ashx.
7. Gallup, *State of the Global Workplace*, 2017. gallup.com/workplace/238079/state-global-workplace-2017.aspx.
8. Weber Shandwick, KRC Research and Institute for Public Relations, *Millennials@Work: Perspectives on Diversity and Inclusion*, 2016. webershandwick.com/news/ millennials-at-work-perspectives-on-diversity-inclusion.
9. Boris Groysberg and Katherine Connolly, "Great Leaders who Make the Mix Work," *Harvard Business Review*, September 2013. hbr. org/2013/09/great-leaders-who-make-the-mix-work.
10. Sujin Jang, "Cultural Brokerage and Creative Performance in Multicultural Teams," *Organization Science* 28 6 (November–December 2017): 965–1167, C2. doi.org/10.1287/orsc.2017.1162.
11. Boris Groysberg and Katherine Connolly, "Great Leaders who Make the Mix Work," *Harvard Business Review*, September 2013. hbr. org/2013/09/great-leaders-who-make-the-mix-work.

1. Interview with the author.
2. Michael E. Porter and Nitin Nohria, "How CEOs Manage Time," *Harvard Business Review*, July–August 2018. hbr.org/2018/07/the-leaders-calendar.
3. "Patagonia: Yvon Chouinard," *How I Built This with Guy Raz*, National Public Radio, December 25, 2017. npr.org/2018/02/06/572558864/patagonia-yvon-chouinard.

CONCLUSION

1. Bruce Rosenstein, *Living in More Than One World: How Peter Drucker's Wisdom Can Inspire and Transform Your Life*. Oakland, CA: Berrett-Koehler Publishers, 2009.

ACKNOWLEDGMENTS

I
T TAKES A village to write and publish a book, and this one is no exception. Although my name is on the cover, many people have contributed to bringing my initial idea onto the page.

I am first and foremost grateful for all my past and present coaching clients, whose stories I hope will inspire and move you the way they have inspired and moved me. Thank you for your confidence, trust, and willingness to be open. Working with you is a privilege and a joy, as well as an endless source of wonder and learning.

Very heartfelt thanks to coach extraordinaire Marshall Goldsmith and his MG100. Thank you, Marshall, for making me part of this extraordinary group of people, for all that you teach us, and for your unwavering support. Your generosity, expertise, and talent make an enormous difference in the world—and in my life. Thank you also for writing the foreword to this book, as well as for your feedback and encouragements.

This book was born out of an article I wrote for *Leader to Leader.* That article—and therefore this book—could not have been written without Frances Hesselbein and Bruce Rosenstein. Thank you both for your support.

Jim Citrin and Tasha Eurich supplied a good dose of inspiration and encouragement to help me get started. Thank you for listening and for your suggestions.

Gregory Enjalbert, Aicha Evans, Philippe Grall, Hubert Joly, Darek Lenart, Jennifer Paylor, and Gregory Renard have been extremely generous in sharing their experience, thoughts, and time with me. You have made this book much richer than it would otherwise have been. Thank you.

Thank you Jeremy Coffman, Tasha Eurich (again!), Hubert Joly (again!), Maude Julien, and Krishna Patel for reading drafts and providing invaluable feedback at various stages of writing. I am grateful for your insights and perspective.

Who would have thought that publishing could be so painless and fun? Thank you Jesse Finkelstein and the entire team at Page Two for your phenomenal support and professionalism. Special thanks to Crissy Calhoun, Peter Cocking, Taisha Garby, Taysia Louie, Gabi Narsted, Paul Taunton, Annemarie Templeman-Kluit, and Lorraine Toor. You rock!

Special thanks to Elysabeth Bastoni, Pierre René Lemas, Fiona Macaulay, Daniel Mayran, Philippe Mercier, Scott Osman, Bertrand Richard, Bernard Spitz, Francois Van Aal, and Kathy Wolff.

Caroline Lambert knew how to perfectly translate my thoughts into these pages, thanks to her writing talent, her ability to listen, her ideas, her professionalism, and her unshakable positivity. Thank you, Caroline, for creating this alignment and this journey, and for all the fun we had along the way!

Lastly, I owe a lifelong debt of gratitude to my children, Greg and Charlotte, and my parents, Bernard et Marie-Françoise le Gentil. I would not be who I am without your love and support.

And all my gratitude to YOU, my reader. I hope *Aligned* helps you find the best *you*!

ABOUT THE AUTHOR

HORTENSE is an Executive Leadership Coach and the President and Founder of JAY Consulting. She works with decision makers in the business world, including many C-suite executives from Fortune 500 companies, supporting them in their development and leadership by working with them on the alignment between their personal values and their professional activities.

Prior to coaching full time, le Gentil spent over 30 years in business in various industries, working for leading multinational companies in the areas of media consulting, marketing, and advertising. She then founded and spent 10 years as CEO of an entrepreneurial start-up (in metals recycling).

Hortense is part of the MG100 Coaches, Marshall Goldsmith's Pay It Forward project, and is a certified Marshall Goldsmith Stakeholder Centered™ Coach. She has been selected to receive a Thinkers 50 coaching award for excellence in her field. She is the author of several articles about leadership and coaching in such publications as Leader to Leader and Les Echos.

Working with Hortense was very enlightening. Through listening, understanding, and a dash of authority, she helped me understand a leader's responsibilities to their employees, the difference between what a leader should be doing and what I was actually doing, and how to close that gap in order to become a better leader. Thus the leader is indeed a person with contradictions, aspirations, and values; all of this must be aligned, for reasons of efficiency, the leader's well-being, their employees, and their company. Hortense monitors this and brings an element of harmony and trust which is inseparable from performance.

CEO OF A MAJOR FINANCIAL SERVICES COMPANY

CPSIA information can be obtained
at www.ICGtesting.com
Printed in the USA
LVHW011800180120
643992LV00002B/40

CPSIA information can be obtained
at www.ICGtesting.com
Printed in the USA
LVHW011800180120
643992LV00002B/40